CHRISTIAN
COMMUNICATION
RECONSIDERED

CHRISTIAN COMMUNICATION RECONSIDERED

John Bluck

WCC Publications, Geneva

Cover design: Rob Lucas

ISBN 2-8254-0975-8

© 1989 WCC Publications, World Council of Churches,
150 route de Ferney, 1211 Geneva 2, Switzerland

Printed in Switzerland

Contents

Introduction

To attempt a book on Christian communication is outrageous from the outset. It's a subject best left to mystics and musicians to take care of by doing rather than defining.

But like it or not, Christian communication has entered the index of respectable subjects to define and footnote, to enrol in and build careers on. And after all, the subject is no more outrageous than the attempt to make theology systematic. So why not a book on understanding Christian communication, provided it doesn't pretend to guarantee greater success and better results in making faith transparent and attractive? To pretend that would be to leave God out.

Perhaps the most important assumption made in this book is that Christians have no immunity from the difficulties involved in any and every communication process. The quality of grace that makes Christian communication distinctive is beyond our control or influence. Like everyone else, Christian or not, we have to proceed as if it all depends on our integrity and hard work, even though we know that's not enough.

So we need the best information and analysis available on how communication happens, recognizing that the mystery of dialogue with God in Christ will often as not elude our knowledge and skill as communicators. But that's not a reason for being less than expert. It only serves to make our expertise a little less arrogant.

The book grew over a five-year period out of communication studies courses designed for students at the Theological Hall, Knox College, Dunedin. The students are a varied bunch. Mostly older women and men, having worked as everything from farmers to factory hands, many of them immigrants from Pacific Island countries. All are aware that communication is a crucial issue in Christian ministry.

But how do you begin to address such a huge subject? The book simply suggests some starting points that have proved helpful in this New

Zealand setting. It's introductory only, but even so, determined to go beyond the mechanical, how-to-do-it mentality of so many current books on communication. This book argues that skills without understanding and technique without theology are cold comfort to people who want to become more credible communicators.

1
What is Communication?

Even the simplest definition of communication invites an argument. But the invitation is rarely taken up, for different communication disciplines spend more time specializing than sharing their understandings. Let's begin then by listing some of the starting points that different disciplines provide.

The word communication comes from the Latin *communis* (common) and *communicare* (to establish a community, to share). So from the outset there's something corporate involved. Some sort of interchange or dialogue is demanded in communication, unlike information which may or may not be exchanged and shared.

Theologically, communication begins and ends with that dimension of dialogue. The opposite of communication, argues Michael Traber, is not silence but sinfulness — the refusal to be in communion.[1] Sin is everything that prevents or distorts communication, symbolized by the devil who in biblical terms is the liar. Communication, as a theological word, becomes an issue of right relationship with God and each other, presupposing dignity, equality and freedom.

The danger of such definitions is that they can become a moralist's delight, leading to quick judgments rather than clear analysis. The Christian community is better at exhorting the value of good communication than coping with the complexity of communication break-downs. A moralistic view of communication leaves us looking for someone (like the devil) to blame for failure. A multi-disciplined approach helps us see the true intricacy and sense the real mystery of any communication process.

Historically, communication has determined the speed and direction of social change and hence formed the location of enormous power, once

---

[1] John Bluck, *Beyond Technology*, Geneva, WCC, 1984, p.61.

held by the poets and priests of traditional societies and now by the magnates and gatekeepers of modern electronic media.

Shaun McBride in the introduction to the UNESCO report offers a definition that leaves little out:

> Communication maintains and animates life. It is also the motor and expression of social activity and civilization; it leads people and peoples from instinct to inspiration, through variegated processes and systems of enquiry, command and control; it creates a common pool of ideas, strengthens the feeling of togetherness through exchange of messages and translates thought into action, reflecting every emotion and need from the humblest tasks of human survival to supreme manifestations of creativity — or destruction. Communication integrates knowledge, organization and power and runs as a thread linking the earliest memory of man to his noblest aspirations through constant striving for a better life. As the world has advanced, the task of communication has become ever more complex and subtle — to contribute to the liberation of mankind from want, oppression and fear and to unite it in community and communion, solidarity and understanding. However, unless some basic structural changes are introduced, the potential benefits of technological and communication development will hardly be put at the disposal of the majority of mankind.[2]

The debate over how to bring about those "basic structural changes" has become one of the most savage international political issues of the decade, with a few member states punishing UNESCO for the way it presented the issues. The search for a new international communication order that challenges the privilege and power of established media systems, whether capitalist or communist, seems as elusive as the search for a new economic order to redistribute the world's wealth.

Like theology, history and politics help us see how important communication is but don't pretend to explain how it happens. We look for that explanation in the disciplines of social science.

The search will lead us into some technical and often mechanical explanations. They seem to offer a precision which in fact doesn't exist because communication is always a dynamic, fluid and ever-evolving process. The social sciences help us chart those changes but the course they chart crosses an ocean of unknown size and boundaries. "All communication is interpretation," says John McQuarrie. "It takes place when some aspect of the shared work is lit up and made accessible to both parties in the discourse."

---

[2] On the New World Information and Communication Order, *Many Voices, One World*, Kogan Page/Unipub/Unesco, p.3.

Such a transaction of lighting and opening up is a very inexact, hit-or-miss affair. Communication is more a matter of holding up lots of candles in a great darkness and hoping some light reaches a mostly invisible audience. That should be the context for reading the technical considerations that follow.

Technically, at its simplest, communication is a matter of offering something in order to draw a response that can be shared between (or within) us. There has to be, quite literally, a giving and a taking, for communication to happen.

Invariably that "taking" or receiving dimension is underplayed. Take the widely held belief that communication is a matter of senders "giving" messages that convey meanings to receivers. And of course the bigger, louder, glossier, more frequent the message, the clearer the meaning, goes the argument.

But the reality is quite different. Meaning is something that only we ourselves can give to the message we receive. No matter how eloquently or authoritatively the message is presented, its meaning depends on how we decode it and value it. And if by chance we as receivers end up giving the same meaning to a message as the one intended by the sender, then that's as much, if not much more, to do with *our* skill, knowledge and experience as it is to do with the sender of the message.

Communication is about negotiating messages, not transmitting meanings. It's about meetings, not mail-boxes. The distinction is a vital one as we'll see in more detail when we come to discuss some theoretical models. An understanding of communication as human negotiation rather than mechanical transaction, as relationship to be worked out between at least two partners, that much is essential for our basic definition. But to insist on much more becomes difficult, as John Fiske shows so clearly. He describes two separate approaches to the study of communication — the "process" school and the "school of semiotics" (the science of signs and meanings).

> The first sees communication as the *transmission of messages*. It is concerned with how senders and receivers encode and decode, with how transmitters use the channels and media of communication. It is concerned with matters like efficiency and accuracy. It sees communication as a process by which one person affects the behaviour or state of mind of another. If the effect is different from or smaller than that which was intended, this school tends to talk in terms of communication failure, and to look to the stages in the process to find out where the failure occurred. For the sake of convenience I shall refer to this as the "process" school.

The second school sees communication as the *production and exchange of meanings*. It is concerned with how messages, or texts, interact with people in order to produce meanings; that is, it is concerned with the role of texts in our culture. It uses terms like signification, and does not consider misunderstandings to be necessarily evidence of communication failure — they may result from cultural differences between sender and receiver. For this school, the study of communication is the study of text and culture.[3]

The "process" school focuses on what happens in any communication act or event. The "semiotic" school is more interested in the end result or product of any communication, however it happened and for whatever reason. Semiotic scholars care more about what was heard and seen to be said, rather than what was intended. That's because they place great emphasis on the power of the wider community and culture to shape the outcome of a communication event.

This is seen most vividly in the way anti-American audiences are able to completely reverse the intended roles of "goodies" and "baddies" in Hollywood movies. A semiotic scholar would accept that reversal and start his or her analysis there, even if the cop or cowboy hero had become the criminal. The process scholar would want to dwell on how that reversal happened and remind us who the hero was really meant to be!

The two schools lend themselves to different areas. The "process" school is helpful for diagnostic or therapeutic purposes. Issues of group dynamics or interpersonal communication draw heavily on process models. Semiotic analysis on the other hand thrives in mass media contexts where connections are hard to make between the individual receiver's experience of the message and the highly complex production of that message for a mass audience.

This book tries to reflect both these schools of communication theory as well as the classical discipline of rhetoric that fits into neither theoretical school. So at least three different points of entry into understanding communication are presented in a very preliminary way.

Yet another approach emerges even as this book goes to press; even more comprehensive than anything discussed here. It is the school that sees communication as "the process of symbolic interaction which creates our cultural environment". That definition became an organizing principle in the World Association for Christian Communication's world congress in Manila, in October 1989.

---

[3] *Introduction to Communication Studies*, New York, Methuen, 1982, p.2.

Culture and communication become two sides of the same coin in this view. Our humanity is bound up in making and sharing symbols. Communication happens when those symbols interact with some effect. Culture is the system of organizing that interaction, the environment for our communication. This environment is as fragile as the natural world. Its preservation and stewardship is an ecological issue.

This "culture and communication" approach, developed at the WACC congress, though long familiar in many regional settings, promises to dominate the ecumenical debate and bring new insights to the much broader ecumenical theme of "justice, peace and the integrity of creation".

The same approach should help us also in seeing connections between the study of communication and theology. Because for our purposes in this book, the final choices are theological. That is, they are tested against gospel values and choices — the dignity given to people, the respect for incarnation, the space made for mystery and surprise. Some communication theories constrain those choices and values. Others help us develop a communication theology, along the lines suggested in the last chapter of this book.

2
How it Works

Neatly drawn, with elaborate explanations, communication models pretend to pin down communication and make it precise, measurable and manageable. We know it's not so. All we offer with a model is a small attempt to fabricate an explanation of an event and its outcome that are extremely imprecise and largely unmanageable. Communication is always shaped by many more variables than we can see or control, most of what matters bounces off the walls or is built into the furniture. What's more, it is always a multi-levelled, repetitive and circular process impossible to draw in any static outline. So the drawings that follow may project a confidence they don't deserve. That confidence is not surprising, given the scientific and technological origins of much communication theory. For instance, Shannon and Weaver's *Mathematical Theory of Communication* published in 1949, and their wartime engineering work in the Bell telephone laboratories, have greatly influenced the communication models we work with today. In communication studies we frequently find ourselves applying models from high technology to human processes, fitting language from mass media to personal relationships. The matching of model to situation is crucial then, for communication events can range from electronic mass media engaging millions to inter- and intrapersonal communication where the dialogue is entirely within.

Whatever the event, there are some common elements. Harold Lasswell summarized them succinctly:

who — says what — in which channel — to whom — with what effect

That model fits almost any communication event, but how do we represent it in diagram form:

as spirals

interlocking circles

or circles within circles

linear projections

ripples out and back

triangular forms

sets and sub-sets

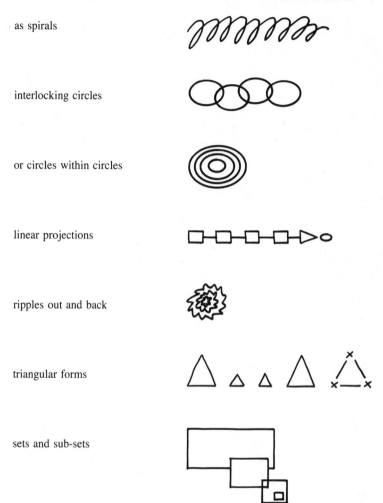

All these and dozens more options have been used to represent the complexities of the communication process.

So Riley has used the sub-sets to show the importance of primary groups:

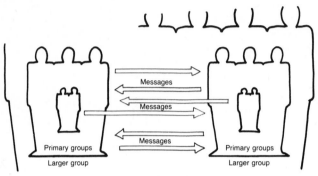

The ripple effect is used in the Hub model to show the gate-keeping, coding, packaging, filtering mechanisms of mass media.

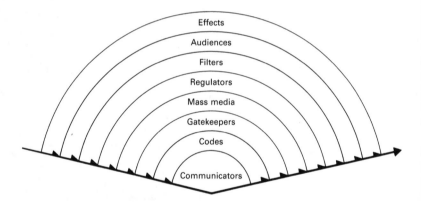

The linear projection by Shannon and Weaver shows the encoding and decoding involved in any signal reaching its destination.

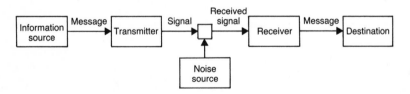

The interlocking circles by Wilbur Schramm show how messages depend on sender and receiver.

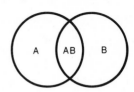

The triangle by everyone from

Aristotle 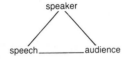 to Newcomb

The helical model by Dance shows the dynamic nature of the process.[1]

The most favoured form, however, remains the circle, especially if you can draw it three-dimensionally, for it comes closest to catching the over-and-over, yet onward-and-onward nature of the communication process.

David Berlo's model gives us a good place to start and develop the diagram that best serves the kind of communication situation or event we want to analyze.[2] But whatever the diagram, the following components will be involved: Source, Message, Channel, Receiver, Feedback.

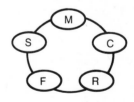

---

[1] For a detailed description of these and other models, see Denis McQuail and Sven Windahl, *Communication Models for the Study of Mass Communication*, New York, Longman, 1982.

[2] See Merrill Abbey, *Communication in Pulpit and Parish*, Philadelphia, Westminster, 1973, ch. 2.

Source (also sender, speaker, encoder, actor, communicator)

Traditional communication theory has made much of source by listing the virtues of good character, will and sense. Effective communication with this focus hinges on the credibility, reputation and moral worth of the speaker. The orators of classical Greece and Rome and today's talk-show hosts, newsreaders and TV evangelists illustrate the seemingly unlimited power of the sender to shape the communication circle. But the components that follow will show that source power isn't as great as it seems, however popular, visible and photogenic the sender may be.

Sources who enjoy high public exposure develop an illusion of communication power and influence that seems limitless. Moon landings without Walter Cronkite or famine relief without Bob Geldorf is inconceivable.

More important than the moral worth, physical beauty, hypnotic power or whatever else about the source is the degree to which he or she relates to the receiver. It's the depth of that relationship that is all-important; the degree to which a receiver can identify with source. It may not be a relationship of great health or goodness; it may be dependent, dehumanizing and distasteful, but relationship it surely is. How the source understands it and sustains it are more helpful questions than searching for some inherent gift or advantage built into the source.

Message (also content, signal, intention)

This is never, never, never to be simply equated with *meaning* which is an altogether different, receiver-dependent thing. One message always contains a myriad of meanings. What, rather than how or by whom, is the question here. The message is a set of symbols organized to draw a particular response. The big question of course is whether we define message by the response that source *intended* or the response that the receiver in fact made. There could be all the difference in the world. Our earlier discussion requires us to consider both possibilities.

"Words are maps not territories," linguist S.I. Hayakawa reminds us, and in that sense precision about intentions, or outcomes, is impossible. So we settle for negotiating approximations, taking into account all the evidence we can find. But the final definition of message is settled by whatever was "received and understood", to borrow the classic phrase from radio telephone transmission. All the components of the communication circle will contribute to that reception but it's the receiver rather than the sender who has the final say in defining the message. That's a very arbitrary claim. Some would argue message is more to do with sender or medium, which as Marshall McLuhan argued *is* the message. But in the theology section of this book we'll make a case for the receiver having the last word.

All this only adds to the difficulty of defining message, except as a source's best intentions, and there's little value in them alone. The road to hell is paved with them, so we're told. For any message to have wider use it has to be "encoded" by source — translated into language, symbols, sequence and shape that has some hope of being shared and understood. Message then has to be "decoded" by a receiver.

To talk about message apart from this decoding and encoding activity is about as helpful as setting out, like Winnie the Pooh, to capture some mythical Hefalump.

To decide whether a message exists apart from the language and symbols that carry it is a philosophical task beyond our scope here. But for the purpose of better understanding a communication event, message is best defined as including the form of encoding and decoding that must always accompany it. If it's encoded in a way that makes it difficult or demeaning for the receiver to understand, or in a way that inflates the importance of source, then that becomes part of the message. Several factors govern this en- and decoding, but among the most powerful are operative image and knowledge levels.

An "operative image"[3] is the association evoked by an object, word, or symbol in any given receiver. Such images need to be carefully researched for they create powerful blocks or openings for communication. Deeply held convictions about what's glamorous, funny, sacred, sexy, outcast, etc., are expressed through these mental pictures. Abbey argues that a communicator needs to know four things about any images to be used:

— Its clarity — how well defined and focused is the association?
— Its salience — how readily or easily is it triggered?
— Its coherence — how well does the association hang together? Does it contain dissonant elements?
— Its integration — how does it integrate with other images held by the receiver? Does it harmonize or clash with them?

The answers to those questions determine the sender's choice of images and help in building a communication strategy that has some chance of results. Encoding messages in images that don't understand and respect the receivers' present associations and their distinctive patterns and contours, strengths and weaknesses will result in senders talking only to themselves.

---

[3] *Ibid.*, pp.59f.

Knowledge level is another key consideration in selecting and shaping a message. Unless we begin with some clarity about what the receiver already knows, needs and understands, our message is going to risk being superfluous and irrelevent at best, insulting and demeaning at worst. Abbey uses Theodore Clevenger's series of questions to establish this knowledge level:

a) Does the audience know a problem exists? The classic example is provided by evangelists who with great conviction offer Christ as the answer, but are much less clear about what question they're answering, or even whether anyone is asking it.

b) How has the audience formulated the problem? Very often messages preclude this formulation by prejudging it. "How can I help you unfortunate people?"

c) How much information does the audience have, and have all the alternatives been considered?

d) What criteria will the audience apply to decide what's appropriate/ successful/dignified/practical, etc. What's technologically practical may be culturally offensive. Cross-cultural studies abound in stories of communities that were "improved" and modernized at the cost of their identity and dignity.

e) Has the audience committed itself on the question? What people know, like and feel confident about forms the base line for filtering, accepting or ignoring new messages.

Communication only produces change when that pattern of existing loyalties is respected, its points of weakness, uncertainty or indifference identified and understood.

This discussion of knowledge levels and operative images could equally well be discussed under the heading of receiver, but we locate it here to challenge the tendency, especially in church circles, to understand message in general, universal terms, dissociated from receiver or channel, as if there's some objective reality to message quite independent of how it's received and understood. Such a view is misleading, for even the eternal "message" of Jesus' teaching is incarnated in the cultural context of his experience and that of the community who gathered around him and passed on his story.

Channel (also medium, means, form, context, culture, transmitter, vehicle)

Narrowly technical definitions of this component are disastrous, for the channel can be as broad as the whole culture that surrounds us or as precise as a transistor radio set. It can be a primary or secondary means of conveying a message, formal and well-recognized or very informal and hidden. Current research gives increasing place to the power of these less prominent channels as receivers are found to rely more on messages that are built into the woodwork, bounce off the walls, or seep between the lines than the officially approved and prominently displayed messages we're expected to receive, absorb and obey.

Channels then are always multi-levelled or working in multiple sets, even in the most straightforward settings. A preacher who thinks his or her voice, gestures and text are the only channels operating would be surprised to learn that such obscure details as the height and ornateness of the pulpit, the memory of earlier sermons and the drooping heads of people in front are at least equally influential channels in conveying the message.

In every channel, certain assumptions are built in, shaped by how the audience is defined and the predominant use of that channel. Whose faces has the channel grown accustomed to? What kind and style of message does it usually carry? These built-in assumptions are what Abbey calls "contemporary axioms" and every separate channel has its own distinctive set, not only newspapers as different from radio, but each different radio station and newspaper. These axioms are strong enough to filter out and dissolve away any message that doesn't "fit" the channel in question. For example, anything that isn't in some way entertaining has a hard time surviving on television, anything that's funny has a limited future in most academic journals, anything that's sexy won't last in a parish newsletter.

So powerful are these axioms that Judith Williamson[4] argues they take on the force of human passion and political ideology, built into the shape and form of consumer product or human body. Because of these axioms or expectations, a channel wrongly used or selected can radically alter, over-ride or even overturn a particular message, as the American electronic church has found with its take-over of the TV talk-show format. The message intended is (hopefully) one of selfless, sacrificial servant-hood and surrender to the mystery of God's love and grace. Yet the channel's axioms speak of success and comfort, consumer satisfaction and easy explanations for everything with bright lights and big smiles.

How do you avoid such channel-related contradictions? One approach is to ensure that personal messages are only conveyed by personal

---

[4] *Consuming Passions: the Dynamics of Popular Culture*, Boyars, 1987.

channels. So face-to-face encounter becomes the only authentic channel for evangelism. Colin Morris explores that option in his book *God-in-a-Box*,[5] but to follow his logic to the limit, and he doesn't, would make his job as the director of BBC mass media religious programmes redundant.

To widen the discussion we turn to social anthropologists. Edward T. Hall's *Beyond Culture*[6] is especially helpful with his distinction between high and low context culture.

A high context culture, common in traditional societies, carries most information in either the physical environment or internally in the people themselves. Very little is explicit or accessible to outsiders. Low context cultures by comparison, while more complex in their technology, tend to make information more accessible and external. An airline timetable is lower context than the protocol for a Maori marae welcome. The instructions on a voting paper or an income tax form in terms of language, position, layout and design are meant to be the simplest and lowest context channel possible. But bureaucrats have a gift of raising, not lowering any context, which usually results in someone having to be around as a back-up channel to explain what the instructions really mean.

Hall's work is also useful in opening up the complexity of forms that any one channel can involve. For example, much communication is carried through rhythm and movement, revealed in the study of synchrony — the science of moving together. So the gesture exchanged, mostly unconsciously in conversation, the distance between people as they talk, the kinesthetic movement of our bodies that affects everything from the speed of our metabolism to the rhythms we respond to in music, speech and visual imagery — all these are vital elements in shaping whether and what communication takes place. It's easy to see in young children's play, old lovers' gestures, shearing gangs and ice skaters, but synchrony applies to all of us. For it is by means of our relationship with the environment — how we move with each other and more broadly with time and space — that communication happens. Different cultures move in different ways is Hall's constant theme. Some to a monochronic (M) time in linear, regular sequence, some to a polychronic (P) time where several things are allowed to happen at once, not always in neatly ordered patterns. And when M time people try to communicate with P time people, confusion is guaranteed.

These elements of the context or culture make communication the exciting process that it is, because, as Hall explains, it is from the context

---

[5] Collins, 1986.
[6] New York, Anchor/Doubleday, 1976, pp.79f.

that we find the missing pieces that cause confusion; pieces that are innate, built into history and place, and accessible only through intuition, memory and imagination. For anyone interested in communicating faith, what could be more important?

A final term that throws light on what channel involves comes from the study of rhetoric where the concept of a "community of discourse" is used to describe the social group that determines who can join a conversation, and measures the credibility of what is shared.

It might take the form of geographical neighbourhood or an ethnic, occupational or age group, but it is usually an invisible community of interest where membership is taken for granted. Such an alliance or network is itself a community and unless both sender and receiver respect it and are somehow attached to it, communication doesn't happen.

Receiver (also destination, decoder, audience, consumer-perspective)

Communications research traditionally painted receiver as passive recipient. Today that picture has been reversed as we appreciate just how powerfully receiver determines whether or not *any* communication takes place. Cross-cultural studies show how receiver can defy and even reverse the message intended by the strongest sender. In consumer cultures, receivers have developed decoding systems as self-protective mechanisms so TV adverts are used for light relief and brands that exploit women, demean ethnic groups or treat us as simpletons promote products at their peril. Certain soap powders have become cultural outcasts as a result.

Yet literature on communication still paints the receiver very much from the view of the sender, for much of the research was motivated by war-time propaganda programmes and subsequently by the advertising industry's equally urgent need to persuade. So questions about the receiver focus on how persuadable is he/she, where are his/her loyalties, how well does the message appeal to basic needs for security, esteem and respect, love, freedom, hope, recognition, community, etc.

The last question especially reflects the military influence on understanding the receiver, for numerous wartime studies have shown that the morale level of a particular military community is a major determinant of members' willingness to accept new information. The lower the morale, the more vulnerable they are to messages that suggest some new loyalty or unfamiliar direction.

The problem with all these questions about the receiver is that they pay little respect to the dignity, distinctiveness and freedom of the consumer. Market researchers have to treat people as objects — to be measured in order to be better predicted and controlled. Western media systems have long cultivated a myth of objectivity that plays down the power, let alone the right, of the receiver to rearrange, resist and refuse the messages sent. The unspoken assumption is that whatever mass media see fit to print or broadcast deserves to be taken as serious and fair. Any debate about that, if it's allowed at all, is strictly on the terms of the sender.

What's needed is a communication model that puts the receiver in the centre of the circle, makes his or her human dignity and worth non-negotiable and then holds all the other components of the circle accountable to that end.

There are good theological arguments for such a priority from a faith that sees salvation as losing self in the service of others. There are also good pragmatic grounds for never underestimating the power of the receiver to make or break, start or stop a communication process.

Psychologists' work on the nature of perception explains the basis of this power. "Perception is primarily the modification of an anticipation," said J.R. Belloff. What we see and hear is conditioned by what we expect, so it becomes impossible to receive any message without some preparation or pre-understanding. J.G. Davies illustrates this dramatically[7] with stories of art works that mean nothing when transferred outside their home cultures. So ornaments become idols, familiar faces go unrecognized in unfamiliar forms of portrait painting, and most vividly in New Testament terms, Jesus walks unrecognized in the Easter morning garden. What we don't expect, we don't see and hear. There has to be what psychologists call "mental set" — a readiness that we've somehow learnt and gathered beforehand. Without it, communication is reduced to cognitive confusion, mental breakdown, even physical revulsion. Disclosure by sender, whether human or divine, requires recognition by receiver. Without it there is no communication.

Feedback (also response)

But feedback is more than response. It's not like a form you fill in and mail off without much expectation of any reply, but rather a response made *in order to* influence any further transmissions or messages. Given the circular nature of the communication process that sort of feedback is being given continually and the communication circle is modified as a result. This ongoing reshaping and retuning by the responses from sender and receiver alike forms the very nature of dialogue.

---

[7] *Everyday God*, London, SCM, 1973.

What more can we say about how these responses work? Firstly that they move through several progressions, as this diagram in Gavin Reid's book *The Empty Pulpit*,[8] makes clear:

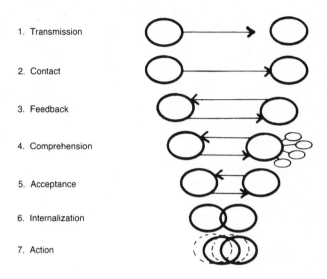

1. Transmission

2. Contact

3. Feedback

4. Comprehension

5. Acceptance

6. Internalization

7. Action

Feedback in the context of this diagram is reduced to an almost preliminary stage on the way to any change in behaviour, understanding and commitment. It underlines the fact that feedback in the sense of some visible response is not enough.

These different levels of response are governed by selectivity mechanisms that enable us as receivers to filter all incoming messages, prevent overload and deal with those we choose to follow up. Davison[9] sees four principal factors governing the selection:

Habit. On the basis of experience we become accustomed to exposing ourselves to some communications and not others.

Consistency. We have a tendency to favour communications that are congruent with our existing ideas over information that conflicts with our mental map of the world.

---

[8] New York, Harper & Row, 1967, p.21.

[9] Phillips Davison, Jas. Boylan and Frederick T.C. Yu, *Mass Media: Systems and Effects*, New York, Praeger, 1976, p.154.

Utility. We select communications that we think will be helpful in satisfying some need, or that will give us pleasure.

Availability. If we have no preference for one communication rather than another, we will expose ourselves to the one that is more easily available.

The order of importance will differ depending on the communication event. In church life for example, utility is usually seen as a source of selfishness, but a high premium is given to consistency. In the current economic debate, that order of preference is reversed!

These selectivity mechanisms are never governed simply by individual choice. As Riley's model showed earlier, the primary groups we belong to (family, work, leisure, etc.) shape our response for we are responding, usually unconsciously, on their behalf as well as our own. Clear communication demands a high degree of coherence and consensus from all components of the process. As receivers we come with all our tribes around us, "trailing clouds of witnesses", knowing that their approval is needed if our feedback response is to be credible and sustainable. In this way feedback is a multiple exercise, an amalgam of yes, no and maybes, our own and those of the groups we belong to, evolving through the stages from feedback to action, and demanding review and the right to change our mind as we go.

Because of this multi-levelled nature, feedback is often under-estimated, either by treating it in a formalistic way (say yes or no, sign here, please attend in person) or by assuming it didn't happen, because of silence or absence. But silence or absence can themselves be powerful indicators of feedback. The fact is feedback is *always* present in a communication process. Without it, communication doesn't happen. We can argue over how well it's recognized, how far it develops, but however invisible and subtle, it's feedback that makes the communication circle go round and keep rolling.

Noise

A separate category in some models influenced by technological research, noise simply refers to anything that obstructs or distorts the communication process.

That can be something quite mechanical from an electric switch to the distraction of a pulpit too high, or it can be an equally "noisy" obstruction of a culturally insensitive sender or a receiver who feels patronized and demeaned. Noises then need not to be confined to channels where we usually expect to find them. They are a risk in every part of the communication circle.

There is however a sense in which noise is an unhelpful concept in communication theory and best left out of the model. If we see communication as a matter of constant negotiation, a relationship that needs continual renewal, a dialogue that demands risk, vulnerability and self-critical review then "noise" seems an odd word indeed in such a context. If we see communication as dependent on the mystery of grace as it is on adjusting the channel and checking the compatibility of encoding and decoding mechanisms, then there is a point where the vocabulary of technology misleads rather than describes.

The communication circle is so complex and fragile that much communication, perhaps most of the time, doesn't happen and only fragments of messages are received. Effective communication is the exception, not the norm. Against such a background, noise, no matter how loud, is a concept that trivializes what's at stake.

Check list

Here in summary form are the questions we've found so far that the communication circle poses. Whether and how we answer them will determine the credibility of our communication.

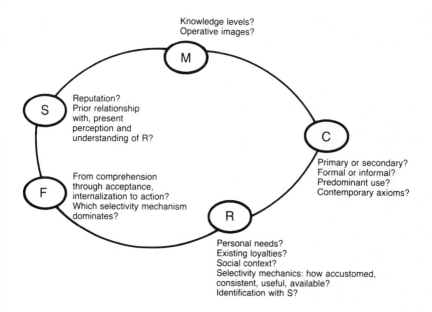

Knowledge levels?
Operative images?

M

Reputation?
Prior relationship
with, present
perception and
understanding of R?

S

C

Primary or secondary?
Formal or informal?
Predominant use?
Contemporary axioms?

From comprehension
through acceptance,
internalization to action?
Which selectivity mechanism
dominates?

F

R

Personal needs?
Existing loyalties?
Social context?
Selectivity mechanics: how accustomed,
consistent, useful, available?
Identification with S?

3
Semiotics

The model we have just described weights our understanding of communication heavily in favour of the "message transmission" school rather than the "semiotics" approach. So before proceeding further, we need to introduce more fully the radically different understanding that semiotic analysis offers.

As we have seen earlier, semiotics places much emphasis on the power of the social and cultural context to shape what gets communicated, regardless of what we intend as sender or however independent we think we are as individuals.

So message becomes more a matter of what's seen or read, rather than the image or the text provided. For semiotics "the message is a construction of signs which, through interacting with the receivers, produce meanings".[1] By that definition, communication becomes a process that's hard to start and stop and it's even harder to measure its success or failure. (The transmission school, by contrast, can claim to be more precise, because intentions can be stated and checked, and senders can be confidently consulted.)

John Fiske's excellent book provides a comprehensive introduction to semiotics. What follows is only a summary of some basic terms that every student of communication needs. Semiotics sees language as a collection of *signs* organized by *codes* or systems of meaning that a culture or group holds in common. *Sign* has a quite precise reference. It's anything — word, symbol, object or whatever — made up of a signifier (the thing itself) and a signified (that which the thing points to or expresses). The codes that govern the meaning of signs will differ of course from culture

---

[1] *Introduction to Communication Studies,* John Fiske, Methuen, 1986, p.3. The applications of semiotics to advertising is described with great clarity in *Advertising as Communication*, Gillian Dyer, New York, Methuen, 1982.

to culture. A coke bottle for example can signify everything from family fun to Western decadence or even spiritual power, as it did in the movie "The Gods must be Crazy" where Kalahari Bushmen turn such a bottle into a sacred object.

Because of this enormous variety of relationships between signifier and signified, a set of terms has developed to sort out the differences. On one end are the arbitrary or highly *symbolic* signs in which you'd never guess from appearances what is meant. Who would imagine that a teenager's worn and torn jeans are a statement of elegance? On the other end of the scale are *iconic* signs where the signifier bears some resemblance to the signified, as in a photograph, drawing or painting. In between these extremes are *indexic* signs where there's some resemblance though rather more indirect, such as between complexion and health, size and strength. The degree of resemblance becomes a sliding scale. Very ruddy cheeks equals very healthy body, small muscles equals slight strength, etc. All communication is a constant shift up and down this scale with different meanings emerging as we shift.

Any consensus about commonly held meanings depends on rules or conventions that govern our grammar, behaviour, appearance, fashion, tastes in food, music, etc. The meaning we attach to any one sign depends on the meaning we give to a much broader group of signs. The significance of any one word is obviously bound up with meanings attached to a whole range of other words in the same language; the significance of one TV episode depends on its relation to the rest of the series.

In semiotic terms this wider set (of episodes or words) from which we choose one sign is called a *paradigm* and good communication analysis requires us to look as carefully at what a sign was chosen *from* as the chosen sign itself. What is left out often tells as much as what is put in. Any good detective will confirm that approach. The murderer gives himself away by the weapon that was available, but not selected. Paradigms are especially revealing in church-related communication, where the choice of symbol or illustration is dramatically shaped and constrained by the piety of the day.

We pick signs with incredible caution from areas that create spiritual unease, such as wealth or sexuality for example. The range of clothes (or make-up) that a woman might wear to church, or the vocabulary of sexually explicit gestures that might be employed in worship form paradigms from which we select and form new systems of meanings that govern what's acceptable in this particular church.

To work only with paradigms would be to say that anything goes. But every communication event involves choices and the combination of our choices from paradigms makes up sets known as *syntagms*. They contain the ground rules by which we decide what is appropriate, tasteful, reasonable, sensible, beautiful. Syntagms that govern our ability to watch TV or drive safely can be readily analyzed. The syntagms by which people decide which church to attend (or avoid), which relationship to maintain (or let go) are more subtle. Nevertheless, they are still the result of choices that we make, however blindly. The concepts of syntagm and paradigm can help us become aware of and thereby take responsibility for areas of communication that were previously unconscious and instinctive.

So far we've introduced signs made up of *signifiers* and things *signified*, linked in very different ways and chosen from a wide range of signs to form *paradigms*, which in turn are grouped in sets called *syntagms* to provide the rules for how we communicate.

These signs are organized, paradigmatically and syntagmatically, into codes that convey meaning agreed on by a particular group or culture. Semiotics has developed some specialized terms to describe these codes[2] but for our purposes of introduction, only the broadest groupings of code need to be understood. Most important is the distinction between *presentational* codes which are indexical, that is they depend on direct relationship with sender or presenter to communicate anything; and *representational* codes where the message or text can function independently of the sender and his/her context.

Religious communication constantly involves both codes — presentational as in pastor, representational as in Bible and prayer book. Different functions of language need different codes. Factual information usually employs verbal representational codes, emotive or expressive material relies more on (non-verbal) presentational codes. The choice and mixture of codes is a major principle of communication strategy.

A further classification comes from Basil Bernstein's work on *elaborated* and *restricted* codes which he linked to social class[3]. "Tight, closed traditional communities tend to use restricted codes," while "the more fluid, changing, mobile, impersonal type of social relations typical of the modern middle class tend to use elaborated codes, even though they're not confined to such codes."

---

[2] John Fiske, *Introduction to Communication Studies*, New York, Methuen, 1982, p.69.
[3] *Ibid.*, p.74.

Restricted codes convey concrete, corporate, here-and-now experience while elaborated codes express more general, abstract or individualized experience. Again, both codes are crucial. Communities can't be built and nurtured without restricted codes, while individuality needs elaborated codes. The current church growth movement is an exercise in switching from elaborated to restricted codes in order to stress the primacy of group membership and loyalty, subdue individuality and simplify theological complexity.

Two other new terms complete our list of essential concepts, this time originating from the work of Shannon and Weaver in the 1940s. *Redundancy* refers not to unemployment but to that which is predictable and conventional in a message. At least half the content of any communication event is redundant in this sense, serving only to make and keep contact between sender and receiver, to keep the channels open and the "show on the road".

Much feedback is also redundant. A case in point is the paraphrasing technique in counselling where you repeat what you hear to encourage the client and check the accuracy of what's being said. Most of church liturgy and a high proportion of sermons are redundant in the sense they say nothing new or unexpected, but serve to reassure and keep the tradition going. The larger and more varied our audience, the more popular a message, the more redundant it is. A "Coronation Street" or "Dallas" can cope with endless crises per episode, provided they're predictable. But anything out of character too often would send the ratings plunging.

Such a surprise is called entropy — the opposite of redundancy. Anything that is new and unexpected, that hasn't been repeated before in a communication event, is entropic. Isn't that what we value most in media programmes, works of art and personal conversation? Yet entropy has negative connotations. In a technical sense it can mean a lack of heat energy, or a tendency to wither and even disintegrate. Effective communication can cope with very little entropy. We can only cope with unpredictable messages in a context of high predictability. What's new and unfamiliar is only acceptable when it comes well wrapped in the old and familiar. (There's some advice here for worship leaders who insist on introducing new hymns and wonder why congregations won't sing them. G.K. Chesterton in his classic essay "On seeing les Quinze" was talking about the same issue — well before semiotics was a subject — when he wrote: "For the purpose of immediate dramatic effect it is necessary to be conventional, for convention is the meeting place of the emotions of myriads of men.")

With this minimum selection of semiotic concepts and the basic SMCRF model of the communication circle, we can now attempt analysis that will hopefully uncover dimensions of communication that were previously buried and camouflaged from sight. Our concern for uncovering the process and interaction and negotiation of a communication event shouldn't however prevent us from seeing the wood for the trees in our analysis. There are empirical, commonsense elements in any communication event that need to be included in our description. "Content analysis" as it's called takes a message at its face value, counts heads and numbers and cash totals and lets the statistics speak for themselves.

A church service may be the most sensitively negotiated and richly complicated communication experience but the fact that there are only six people in the pews, five of them women, all over 50, is content that has to be included in the communication story we tell.

Content analysis by itself can distort what's happening. To count the numerical balance of women and men in a meeting tells you very little about the inclusiveness of the gathering. That might have more to do with the speed and style of the decision-making process and the way in which power is shared, and seen to be shared.

In our next chapter we'll turn to what is the oldest of all methods of communication analysis, namely the science of rhetoric and its attempt to order the different forms and functions of language. This way of seeing communication nicely complements the semiotic process and content schools we've listed so far.

4
Rhetoric

As the art of persuasive speech, rhetoric has a history of two and a half thousand years from its Athenian and Roman origins. Unlike semiotic analysis, the intention and reputation of the rhetor (or public speaker) and his adherence to traditional form count for everything in this approach. Whether he, the rhetor (never she), made an impact on his audience depended both on his moral worth or reputation and his mastery of a highly developed set of rules governing his choice and arrangement of language.

Those rules formed the basis of a science that dominated higher education until the modern period. The standard medieval syllabus was the trivium made up of Grammar — how to express yourself correctly; Rhetoric — how to express yourself effectively; and Logic — how to express yourself in a coherent and systematic way free of contradictions.

Rhetoric has been the least successful survivor of these three, reduced from the status of noble and essential art to a morally dubious technique of verbal manipulation and excess. Part of the explanation is bound up in the post-Renaissance reaction to any sort of artificiality or excessive flourish in the arts and the quest for a more natural simplicity in everything from religion to architecture. What's more, we know the danger of persuasion divorced from ethics in the political dictators of our own century and the commercial tyranny of mass media. Fashions change in the art of persuasion but the fascination with its secrets lives on in today's political image-making industries, advertising and public relations agencies.

The debate over the morality of this art is as old as the study of rhetoric itself. The content of the subject has shifted from tactics and techniques for public debate to a more analytical, linguistic focus. A famous modern scholar of rhetoric, I.A. Richards, defined it as the "study of verbal understanding and misunderstanding".

Despite the changes, some constants remain — notably the insistence on the importance of looking to the *structure* and *style* of any communication, both for understanding what's happening and in order to evaluate its worth and value.

Structure is the way we order the world in order to understand and manage it. Without this structure (form, design or shape) our experience would be unconnected chaos and any attempt to share it with others would be futile. Semiotic analysis describes the complexity of these structures in so far as they are reflected in the text or end product of any communication event. Rhetoric took an even wider view, seeing structure as including everything from the moral reputation of the speaker to the faithfulness of his or her adherence to some very detailed protocols of speech. As rhetorical study evolved it narrowed its focus on these protocols that governed the *style* of all public communication. Literally, a stylus was a pointed instrument for writing on wax, so style came to mean a "way of writing". But a rhetorician's interest was never simply with technique. Questions of style were always a moral consideration. The search was not only for *effective* communication but equally for *good* communication. As the American poet Robert Frost has put it in our own century: "The style is the man. Rather say the style is the way the man takes himself."

English novelist George Orwell took this claim further when he wrote: "The great enemy of clear language is insincerity... When there is a gap between one's real and one's declared aims, one turns instinctively to long words and exhausted idioms, like a cuttlefish squirting out ink."[1] In this light, the style of our communication becomes a matter for fear and trembling. In our choice and structure of language we are seen to be declaring who we are and what our real intentions might be. Quite literally "we give ourselves away" in the style of our communication. The art of rhetoric has always insisted on this moral perspective, though its application has shifted dramatically from a preference for the ornate and complex to the contemporary preference for clarity and simplicity. "Prose is architecture, not interior decoration, and the Baroque is over."[2]

Much of the elaborate detail of rhetorical study finds little use in our time, but the way it divides all discourse according to the function it serves is still illuminating. What are these basic divisions?

---

[1] *Modern Stylists,* ed. Donald Hall, New York, Free Press, 1986, p.24.
[2] *Ibid.*

Classically there were six forms of rhetoric into which all speech could be organized:

exposition	— explaining, informing
description	— sharing impressions
narration	— telling stories
persuasion	— winning over
argument	— truth through reason

Such a division looks complete enough, but as our earlier discussion of communication theory has shown, much depends on whose perspective we make our analysis from. And what's meat to the sender may be poison for the receiver.

Classical rhetoric is heavily dependent on the sender's experience and intention. The choice and description of forms just listed is determined solely by the sender, regardless of whether the receiver recognizes the intention or finds it appropriate.

So we need some division that takes account of the several perspectives that any communication model has to respect. Linguist R. Jakobson developed a model in the 1950s[3] that ties communication functions to six different perspectives — or "factors" as he called them — the *addresser*, *addressee*, *message* in its *context*, *contact* or channel, *code* or shared meaning system. To each factor Jakobson linked a different function of language.

The *emotive* or expressive function is tied to the addresser or sender. The *conative* or knowing function describes the effect on the addressee or receiver. The *referential* function describes the factual, objective claim made by the content of the message. The *phatic* function (highly "redundant" in semiotic terms) is to keep the channel or contact open, the conversation going, the pages turning or whatever. The *metalingual* function identifies the language code in use. Should we treat this message as a sign from God, an entertainment, or a comment aimed personally? The choice of code will be crucial. The *poetic* function is internal to the message itself, involving the pleasure or distaste created by the structure and appearance of the message, be it bumper sticker or choral anthem.

Jakobson's list is valuable for its comprehensiveness but, because of the theological priority we give in this book to communication from a receiver's perspective we need a set of divisions that starts with the effect of a *message*.

---

[3] John Fiske, *Introduction to Communication Studies*, New York, Methuen, 1982, p.36.

So how might you describe the experience of a communication event through a receiver's eyes and ears?

ordering	inviting	affirming	judging	connecting	farewelling	narrating
exhorting	suggesting	encouraging	challenging	identifying	closing	evoking
declaring	consulting	supporting	questioning	greeting	separating	describing
asserting	enabling	forgiving		acknowledging		informing
	sharing					

All sorts of links with this list and the others we've offered become clear. For example the connecting and farewelling columns express Jakobson's phatic function.

In classical Greece or Rome there was indisputable agreement on where and when each form was to be used, as there still is in every traditional society. But in mobile, pluralistic societies like our own there is no such consensus. Even the most institutional and established senders such as law, medicine, education, church, cannot claim or enforce the right to declare and define communication forms any more. Few agencies in our society dare to settle for or insist on even the one form of communication they have traditionally used (be that sermon or Christmas calendar). So the formula becomes one of mix 'n match — a blend of story-telling, cajoling, formal then tongue in cheek, very personal, now immediate, next nostalgic.

The wider the range of codes, the more chance of connecting with the real breadth of a mass audience.

It's because there is no consensus on when to describe and when to exhort that we need a rhetorical framework broad enough to provide lots of options and clear enough to readily identify the effect language is having on the receiver. We live in a period of history that is "between the times", when world-views and value systems blow about and any certainty about place and identity and style is hard to find. The rhetoric for such a time has to be flexible, temporary, experimental and not too solemn. It needs to start from the effect it has rather than from the authority it would like to claim for itself. It can't afford the luxury of standing on its own dignity or protesting the sincerity and value of its own intentions.

And whatever the choice of rhetorical form, these qualities of style will be sought:[4]

---

[4] This is condensed from a check list of prose style developed at much greater length by F.L. Lucas in his book *Style*, London, Pan, 1964.

Clarity:	is it intelligible to the audiences?
Brevity:	are there excessive, wasteful words and images?
Variety:	how many available options are explored?
Decorum:	is it appropriate to occasion, person, purpose?
Good humour:	is it building goodwill or offence?
Sincerity:	is it truly felt and intended?

Those qualities apply equally to any of the categories we've listed. The more authoritative and directive the category, the more referential the function, the more acute the need to respect these marks of style. Slowly, we're beginning to realize that formal communication, especially in the language of law and government, medicine and the church can afford to be clear, brief, funny and varied without the content being demeaned or trivialized. These marks of style really are universal for all forms of communication in modern Western, English-speaking cultures.

The marks of rhetorical style will be written and ordered very differently in other times and places. The historical evolution of rhetorical fashion makes that clear.

Perhaps the most dramatic switch in rhetorical fashion in church life happened with Augustine in the fifth century. He helped to lead what amounted to a rhetorical revolution by rejecting the precise classical equations that had a rhetorical form designed to go with every conceivable public occasion — from light-weight entertainment to heavy-weight solemnity. The post-Constantine church had found itself already locked into the formal, highbrow end of that scale. That was the price of political recognition and cultural respectability. What Augustine helped to promote was a new and distinctive Christian language, much more popular and concrete than that of other professions and much more passionate and earthy than the Stoic fashion of emotional detachment. The highest mysteries of theology could now be expressed in the lowest style.[5] Former vulgarities were incorporated into the language of Christian piety. From the everyday details of eating, chewing and belching to the sweat and passion of love and suffering — all was now fair game, and expressed with a licence to be as down-to-earth and funny as any secular speaker or writer. The old restraints on sacred language were broken down. The energy released by this new rhetorical freedom was a major impetus for the permeation of Christian faith through every level of European society.

---

[5] Eric Auerbach, *Literary Language and its Public,* Boston, Routledge & Kegan Paul, 1965, pp.31f.

The subsequent history of the church can be told in terms of changing rhetorical forms as each new generation of preachers and missionaries seeks to forge a new contract with the surrounding culture in order to be heard and accepted. When such new contracts are not sought, the tendency has been to stand on the dignity of inherited rhetorical forms, insisting that the forms themselves, like old prayer or hymn books, have the gospel built into the arrangements of words. So rhetorical change becomes as heretical as doctrinal change.

We can't attempt here to trace the full range of these rhetorical shifts, but in post-Reformation Europe, one such revolution is described by F.W. Dillistone.[6] He details the changes in communication form that took place from the seventeenth century as the old symbolic means of communicating faith broke down and new ones took their place. What were they?

> In general the answer was: Forms which proved effective in actual experience to reconcile and re-order human feelings within a coherent symbolic structure. Environmental conditions were new, patterns of work were new, the rhythm of human living was new. The major religious symbols for this new age proved to be a new form of preaching and a new form of musical response. The sermon had been important in Elizabethan and Commonwealth days but it had then consisted mainly in the exposition of scripture and its application to public life. Now the new preacher was the *evangelist*. He was mobile and flexible in his approach. He sought out lonely and rootless individuals wherever they were. He declared to them the way of salvation, a way conceived primarily in terms of the need of the individual soul. He spoke the language of the people and used images familiar to them. He preached with warmth and earnestness and lively comparisons...

George Steiner[7] takes the story of this rhetorical evolution into the twentieth century in a chapter evocatively titled "Retreat from the word". His thesis is that our verbal language is becoming increasingly inadequate to describe the breadth of our experience, and in the area of science and mathematics, progressively untranslatable. The new literacy, he believes, is musical and visual rather than verbal, and for a word-dependent tradition like Christianity, that demands some urgent changes. Steiner himself is not endeared to what's happening with these changes in rhetorical fashion. The mass media and consumer culture, he believes, are diminishing and not simply changing literacy, and the

---

[6] *Traditional Symbols and the Contemporary World,* London, Epworth, 1968, pp.82f.
[7] *Language and Silence,* London, Faber, 1958, pp.30f.

language of politics has become "infected with obscurity and madness".[8]

Neil Postman is equally pessimistic in his study of television's destructive onslaught on literacy and our reading/writing culture, in *Amusing Ourselves to Death*.[9]

Not all commentators are as pessimistic about current rhetorical trends. In fact many argue that the new literacy, musical and visual as it is, coupled with the new freedom that a more informal and varied communication climate brings, allows Christians to share their faith more clearly and fully.

But whether we exploit that new freedom or preserve the old forms, our rhetorical choices will make or break all our communication efforts.

---

[8] *Ibid.*, p.54.
[9] New York, Methuen, 1987.

5
Homiletics

Homiletics is still the most dominant stereotype of Christian communication, even though it's the one that church people most love to hate. A book like this would be incomplete without a chapter on preaching, even if most readers never get near a pulpit. For misused and abused as it is, the sermon remains pivotal in most churches' communication strategy.

The expectations that still surround the sermon are huge. The (usually clerical) authority it assumes and affirms is out of line with the other carefully shared and negotiated expressions of authority in the rest of a church's ministry. Somehow the sermon hangs on, shorter perhaps, but oblivious to the difference it doesn't make. Literally built into the furniture of the church, it stubbornly refuses accountability to questions of how power is shared, where else the gospel is being proclaimed, and who is listening anyway. This chapter attempts to defend the art of preaching, to outline an analysis that both listener and receiver can share, and to suggest some ways of expanding our definition of sermon.

The connections with the last chapter are crucial. It's because our appreciation of rhetorical form is so neglected and our use of rhetorical possibilities so narrow that homiletics is in a state of crisis. We begin this chapter without any apology for such dramatic claims. The issue is not a matter of polishing and fine-tuning pulpit technique. A much more radical analysis is needed if what passes for preaching is going to climb out of the incredible communication crevasse that it's fallen into.

Homiletics — the science of which preaching is the art — needs at least a longer definition to do justice to its central place in the Christian tradition. The truth this science seeks to share is the God we know in Jesus Christ as revealed through the scriptures and the tradition of the church. That task, while absolutely central, is of course shared by all dimensions of Christian ministry, so we must go further to find what is distinctive about homiletics.

Above all else, it's about *proclamation* — public declaration or announcement. Traditionally, that has settled some choices of rhetorical form before we begin. It suggests a raised voice, a heightened presence, and language elevated above the ordinary.

None of that is a necessary part of the definition, for homiletics is equally about a work of art which involves us in an ongoing search for what in the context of present need and past experience is beautiful, harmonious, balanced and appropriate. There is no right and fixed form for any art work, let alone a sermon, however venerated the classic forms of sermon might be.

Next, a sermon is an act that happens on behalf of and is owned by a *community* (which sometimes venerates the act to sacramental heights). The truth being told and interpreted is not some individual's property. It belongs to a tradition and the preacher is accountable to that, through the community of faith that guards and sustains the history.

Finally, and to complement the last point, a sermon is itself a *faith event* in which the preacher's own conviction and witness is on the line each time. You might be able to teach about things you aren't convinced of, but you can't preach about them with any credibility. Helmut Thielicke's question to a preacher is the acid test. "Do we live in the house of our own preaching?" If we are only a part-time resident, it becomes very clear, very quickly.

Public proclamation, art form, community act, faith event: it all sounds like a wide open opportunity and yet homiletics has been narrowed down to the opposite of all those features; diminishing in public appeal, uni- (rather than multi-) form in artistic terms, and increasingly individual rather than communal.

The reasons for that are not all modern. They're bound up in the revolution in rhetorical fashion we described in the last chapter.

The origins of today's sermon, according to the classical scholar Erich Auerbach, are found in the classical model of the diatribe or moralistic declamation. Such a form lent itself well to express the urgency of the kingdom's claims and to set the standards and distance of the new church apart from its pagan surroundings, but it was a poor model indeed for conveying the unconditional nature of the love being offered and the unqualified invitation held out by Christ's body.

The model did change, as we've already seen through Augustine's rhetorical innovations, but that rhetorical reform towards a more immediate, popular, accepting and down-to-earth communication style wasn't helped by the political recognition of Christianity by the Emperor Constantine. Hendrik Kraemer[1] describes this pattern of the faith of a once persecuted minority becoming the established ideology of the empire. And as rigid doctrinal rules began to absolutize this ideology, a denunciation rhetoric of anathemas began to dominate. Communication, says Kraemer, began to be replaced by procedures of excommunication, refutation and liquidation.

Little wonder that the sermon, against this background, became a rhetorical vehicle for doctrinal legislation, moral authoritarianism, hierarchical coercion and all those other things that the medieval church is blamed for perfecting and that we've been protesting against ever since.

The historical picture isn't as simple as that, of course. There were periods of great imaginative and spiritual revival in the art of preaching, notably through monastic orders like the Dominicans and Franciscans, and again in the Reformation when preaching regained a central role in liturgy. Yet time and again the revival and expansion of preaching rhetoric was followed by a hardening of the rhetorical form into moral polemic and doctrinal diatribe.

The nineteenth century saw another revival of interest with a spate of "how to" books and the fashion of printing volumes of sermons as edifying literature. Thankfully that latter fashion has waned, but the "how to" books continue, fuelled by our technological society's desperate search for sure-fire formulas to bring guaranteed results. "Follow these ten rules and your congregation's collections will double." Rhetoric is reduced to sales savvy, proclamation shrinks to propaganda and the credibility of the sermon as art form or faith event evaporates.

We find ourselves caught then between the false options of formulas for bigger, brighter results and the defence of tradition that relies on the authority of a learned clergy, the language of Zion and an elevated one-way delivery where no one answers back.

Such options caricature what a sermon could and should be, given our original definition. If we can revalue the sermon as proclamation that is both art form and faith event, not privately owned but offered on our behalf, it will become obvious that a much wider range of people needs to be involved in the "preaching ministry" than is presently the case.

Let's address the two dominant features that presently imprison the sermon. First its reliance on the language of Zion. That reliance makes

---

[1] *Communication of the Christian Faith*, Cambridge, Lutterworth, 1957, Ch. 2.

sense in a community where biblical literacy is high and the centrality of scriptural authority is taken for granted. But it is always part of the preacher's task to show each time why this Bible being quoted is so important. It's a painstaking task for it involves not only a constant restatement of the Bible's credentials as a source of truth, but also a constant redefining and paraphrasing of biblical language and concepts. That's needed even within the community of faith where a commonly held vocabulary of Zion has to be continually reviewed and developed. The familiar complaint of congregations, in rural areas particularly, is that a preacher moves on, "just as he or she is beginning to speak our language". By that they mean their dialect of the language of Zion and its distinctive blend with their local secular language and the images of their landscape.

If that need to constantly restate and redefine biblical language is true for the church community, it's much more important for any form of evangelistic or outreach preaching where no biblical literacy at all can be assumed. One of the greatest communication ironies of our time is the silly spectacle of so-called mass evangelists who claim to be challenging the secular powers and principalities, all the while talking in a language of Zion that is totally incomprehensible to the audience they claim to be swaying. And the more confident and overt the claim to be "evangelizing", the more slavish the dependency on a conspicuously biblical and religious language.

There is nothing sacred for the church about the language of Zion. In communication terms, it needs to be respected in so far as the community of faith values and relies on it for whatever reason, be it for comprehending faith or holding people together through the common reference it provides.

But a theology of ongoing revelation that sees God present and at work in all creation, a Christology that expects to experience the risen Christ in the present tense, an understanding of Spirit that connects up all our experience through what John V. Taylor has called the "go-between God" — such a theology requires a language of spiritual disclosure that is as utterly contemporary in idiom and image as it is faithful to the tradition that directs it.

Peter Berger has talked of "signals of transcendence" — non-religious pointers to the activity of God through our need for order and hope and humour and play.[2]

---

[2] *The Sacred Canopy*, New York, Doubleday, 1967.

David Weeks has sought a similar idea in his "indicator experiences" such as courageous protest, angry compassion and moral crusade that express the power of God's justice and love.[3]

In literature and art, there are endless examples of what novelist James Joyce called "epiphany" moments, fragments of revelation incarnated in human relationships of the natural world, and through which we are startled into recognition of God.

The language (idiom, images and orders) that carry such contemporary epiphanies, indicators and signals, will often need to be much more personal and popular, more earthy and immediate than church people are accustomed to using. It may strike them as vulgar and inappropriate. But we need to claim such language for preachers, accountable to the Bible and the tradition though it must be, for it is language no less holy than the language of Zion.

In fact, such alternatives may prove to be more "holy" if they help the preacher connect with the inner language of his or her community, that level of discourse that requires us to risk personal vulnerability.

Denham Grierson[4] argues that the greatest challenge of preaching is to tap into that "inner language". Fluency in the "outer" public language of description is no guarantee for it is often a "superimposed" language that doesn't align any more with our experience or trigger our imagination. The language of Zion, Grierson believes, is increasingly relegated to this "superimposed" category, disconnected from our inner vocabulary.

The other feature that bedevils the traditional sermon is its failure to deal with the dynamic of feedback, which as we've seen in our theory section is essential if communication is to take place at all. Numerous studies have shown that the greater the opportunity for feedback, response, discussion and review, the greater the scope and accuracy of learning.

Some critics charge that communication doesn't take place in most sermons, precisely because there is no provision for, or invitation to respond. Such accusations however are often made from a very naive view of feedback, as if to say its presence or absence depends on the permission of the sender.

In fact, the receiver in the communication circle is not so bound. Feedback happens all the time in any event. It's a constant, unstoppable, repetitive process, usually regardless and in spite of the invita-

---

[3] *Doing Theology*, 1957.
[4] *Transforming a People of God*, JBCE, 1984, pp.69f.

tion and opportunity offered by the speaker. Most feedback flows not through officially approved, audible, visible channels, but through the silences and the gaps, under the cover of some seemingly unrelated activity.

The classic example of this feedback in camouflage is the post-sermon handshake at the door of the Sunday morning service. There has been no chance for dialogue or review of what has been preached but the non-verbal responses have filled the silences and bounced off the sanctuary walls long before the benediction was pronounced. And by the time the last of the congregation has filed past the preacher has discovered — from hand pressure, voice tone, facial expression and from what hasn't been said — just what effect the sermon had.

Feedback, then, is never absent, from even the most apparently monological preaching occasion. The challenge lies in respecting the feedback that is already happening and that's best done by giving it space and visibility.

How then can we rethink the sermon to respect what actually happens in the communication process, and to see the receiver as an active participant in, rather than passive absorber of proclamation? Ways of doing that include:

— Creating sermon preparation groups, perhaps connected to an ongoing Bible study group or linking reflection on the lectionary to regular meetings of parish committees, so the task is experienced as a shared one, even if the presentation is still made by a single person. Part of the preparation for next week becomes an evaluation of the last effort with members mandated to consciously gather feedback from others.

— Designating "responders" who make a public, preferably prepared response, as part of the sermon event or immediately following, with tea or coffee.

— Creating space for silence, sometimes with appropriate music, after biblical readings, during and after the sermon and flowing into the intercessions.

— Building opportunity for discussion with neighbour or small group into the service and designing the sermon as a lead into that smaller discussion, perhaps with printed questions and quotes.

— Developing less verbal, more visual, music and movement centred channels as part of the proclamation. This will require greater preparation, careful attention to staging, lighting, timing and coordination, but the more channels employed, the greater the opportunity for feedback.

So far we have undertaken a kind of ground-clearing operation that could help to open up a freer and wider space for the sermon in the total ministry of the church. But within that new setting, sermons through whatever channels, and by whichever preachers, still have to be prepared and presented. What are some more pragmatic guidelines for that task?

To attempt such guidelines drops us into territory equally well travelled by wisdom-bearers and conmen alike, and where the tongue needs to be in the cheek before we begin. Besides, it's all been said before, as this eleventh-century advice from the Persian writer Kaikavus to his son, makes clear:

> Should you become a preacher, you must have the Koran by heart... In the pulpit do not engage in wrangling or debate unless you know that your adversary is weak. But you may make any claim that you wish from there, for there are many questioners around the pulpit but no one who listens to answers. Make your tongue eloquent... only avoid being at a loss for words; and make sure your clothes are clean.
>
> Make sure that loud-cheering disciples of yours are always seated among the audience who shall make a rousing noise and applaud at every point you make and keep the assembly warm. If some of your hearers weep, do you also shed a tear from time to time. Should you ever be at a loss for what to say, let it not trouble you; engage in prayer and recital of the creed. Never be sour-faced, otherwise your congregation may become as heavy of spirit and sour-faced as yourself...
>
> Study your audience constantly; if it demands wit, speak wittily; if stories... in short, let your discourse be anything for which there is popular demand. Once you have won success, fear nothing; offer the worst discourse as though it was the best of all things, for when you have the audience with you they will eagerly buy it. But when you are popular be careful for a preacher's enemies appear when he is popular. Do not remain in a place where you fail.
>
> When questions are launched at you in the pulpit, reply to those to which you know the answer; retort "Such questions are not suited for the pulpit; come to my house so that I can answer you." No one will ever come to the house...
>
> Your appearance should ever be new and unfamiliar; therefore do not dwell overlong in any one city; the livelihood of preachers and fortune-tellers depends on their legs, and their success upon the unfamiliarity of their faces... bid men do only those things which you do yourself; thereby you will show yourself a man of integrity as well as of religious knowledge...
>
> In your sermons let all that you say inspire both fear and hope. Do not allow people to despair completely of God's mercy, nor yet send everyone to paradise without good deeds. In general speak on those matters in which you

are properly versed and of which you have a good knowledge, for the result of unsubstantiated pretence is disgrace.[5]

Few Christian preachers have faced such formidable resistance or been forced to resort to such cynical techniques to survive. But the quote is not as outrageous as it sounds. Much homiletic advice of the how-to-do-it variety is no less pragmatic, assuming that gospel proclamation can be guaranteed if certain public speaking techniques are employed. Sermons become craft not art, with no necessary reference to faith event or originating community.

Are there any guidelines, then, that always apply to the shaping and presenting of any sermon? I'd suggest there are some, though they don't involve allegiance to any particular rhetorical form or even length of time allowed! For the only non-negotiable definition of a sermon is its proclamation mode and its gospel reference or anchor.

Because it is an act on behalf of a community, the choice of sermon form and style will depend on:
— my contract with the receivers (a shared set of expectations and understandings that has to be constantly reviewed and updated);

because it is a gospel proclamation, on:
— my care and respect for the biblical text and the liturgical context;

because it is an art form, on:
— my responsibility for a style that gives clarity, coherence, brevity, variety, humour as we listed earlier;

because it is a faith event, on:
— my obligation to own and anchor the exegesis in the present experience of living in Christ that I share with the community of faith.

As we make our choices of sermon form and style within this framework, we ask the question:

Who speaks best through *what*, *when* and *where*? Each part of the question requires an answer.

Who speaks? Who is best placed to speak here, on this text? Within the community of faith at least, where is the experience and expertise that must be acknowledged and drawn on for credible communication to occur? Perhaps several voices need to be involved and orchestrated together.

---

[5] *Christianity and Crisis*, 4 May 1987, p.157.

Through what? What channel is most appropriate for this text, in this context? That's more than deciding where to stand to speak from. There are choices to be made about verbal forms (testimony, narrative, entertainment, exhortation, lamentation, inspiration, etc.), along with non-verbal forms (dress, colour, light, movement, gesture, music, etc.).

When? What is the best liturgical moment for this sermon, in the flow from thanksgiving, through confession to intercession? How is it best coupled with the reading of scripture? Need the sermon be confined to one slot in the service? There are also questions of internal timing within the sermon, namely the balance between recalling, being present and anticipating. Older and younger, more or less established congregations will expect different mixtures of time past/present and future. Few of us can tolerate spending too much time in the present and the insistence of Jesus that we live fully for this day is hardest of all to follow.

Where (and for whom)? The place itself (how established is the community and its pattern of worship?) sets the expectations and the rules that have to be respected and negotiated, if they are to change. The range of such contexts, even within one denomination, increases by the day — from unvarying tradition to mandatory spontaneity, from the very explicit to the most implicit and subtle proclamation.

How do we measure the care with which these questions have been asked and answered? Here's a check list that we've developed over several years of preaching exercises.

How well was the sermon communicated?
Focus on manner and style of presentation noting such issues as use of voice, speed, delivery, gesture, movement, eye contact, use of notes.

How well was the sermon conceived and structured?
Clarity of intention, development and arrangement of ideas, continuity and flow; does it begin and end well? is it easy to follow?

How well was the sermon anchored?
In personal experience and ownership, in biblical exegesis faithful to the text, in cultural context through appropriate language, images, examples.

Was the audience respected and responsive?
Was this the appropriate message for this audience? Were they given space to choose and draw conclusions? Were they accepted, respected, included? Did they seem to respond?

Sermon construction deserves more explanation, for nothing we've said so far is much help to the preacher in the step-by-step assembly of a sermon. The market is well stocked with this sort of how-to-do-it advice, much of which only serves to deepen boredom when applied as rule of thumb. Start with a text, make three points, end with an exhortation, tell them what you're going to do, then do it, then tell them what you've done. Modern preachers are best left to sprinkle us with the juice of their own imagination than follow such advice.

Maybe it was useful once. It isn't now, in an age when our consciousness is shaped by communication forms, notably through mass media, that don't move in the sequential, rational, authoritative way modelled by most sermons. It's David Buttrick's appreciation of this new communication environment that makes his book *Homiletic — Moves and Structures* so valuable.[6]

He argues that unless we're writing shopping lists or programming computers we don't talk in numbered points or logical lists, but rather in "moves" in a flow of language that patterns understanding by clustering, shifting, spacing and arranging words, ordering the sequence and linking of one idea to another.

It's a fluid business, says Buttrick, involving "naming", "story-telling", and a "symbolic-reflective" aspect (beyond story) where we reflect the character (as opposed to the plot) of being in Christ and his body, the church.

The organizing of these moves is a matter of rhetorical strategy that orchestrates movement — opening and closing, connecting and disconnecting. This orchestration (which Buttrick develops in great detail) is necessary not only at the beginning and end of a sermon, but also for every move in between.

Opening moves are needed to focus consciousness and set the style and pace of what follows. A subtle negotiation takes place here between what the preacher has to offer and what the congregation expects. Hopefully, a shared framework is established.

Closing moves round off, and stop the action, even if that action is deliberately incomplete. Moves that aren't "closed" block whatever new move might follow.

Associating moves link Christian understanding with our experience, showing our faith is "true to life" through likeness and connections, rather than facts and proofs, made via imagery, illustration, example, testimony, etc.

---

[6] London, SCM, 1987.

Disassociating moves, says Buttrick, set our awareness of being saved over *against* our being-in-the-world. The double citizenship of every Christian is employed to seek out contradiction, exception, resistance, denial and dissimilarity. Such moves speak to the yes-but, already-not-yet, in-but-not-of experience of faith.

These then are four basic rhetorical strategies. What rhetorical resources are available to the preacher in developing these moves? They can be roughly divided into issues of language choice and use, and issues of stance and point of view.

Language: Our study of rhetoric has shown how preachers favour certain *modes* of language — exhortation over description, inspiration rather than entertainment or lamentation, in the mistaken belief that proclamation requires raised voice, brave challenge and a very personal declaration.

Also involved is a choice of vocabulary. The issue here is not how extensive or specialized, as in the language of Zion or the jargon of professional theology, but rather one of simplicity, cultural appropriateness and what Buttrick calls "connotative" power. "If a sermon is well spoken, we can visualize, think, feel, and, therefore understand on many levels at once."[7]

The third and most overlooked issue of language concerns the *rhythm* or cadence of words — the way they rise and fall and flow depending on both sound and syntax; in repeated, doubled and tripled patterns, spaced, paused, paced faster and slower. Our collective sense of what rhythm is appropriate to the pulpit is more discerning than we realize. It's not the same as the rhythm of a printed page, or a private conversation or a schoolroom lesson. To catch onto the appropriate rhythm has the power to make an otherwise ordinary sermon extraordinary, or to reduce brilliant material into bordeom.

Point of view: If language choices have been reshaped by the mass media culture, conventions about points of view have been revolutionized. Film, radio, television and now electronic data processing and satellite links take it for granted that we are willing and able to process new information and see the world from no fixed viewpoint. Ten minutes in front of the TV might switch you visually and verbally from the experience of a starving Ethiopian child to a wholesale carpet salesman, from the official stance of authority to those on the receiving end, from first person testimony to third-person detachment, from talking to being talked to and talked about.

---

[7] *Ibid.*, p.189.

Where we stand to speak, and how close and with what perspective —
all the things that shape consciousness (mine, yours, ours) keep switching
in almost every form of modern communication, except the pulpit. There
an effort is still made to speak objectively and authoritatively on behalf of
the whole church about the whole world, with occasional lapses into first
person testimony that makes the preacher, rather than the gospel, the
focus.

The challenge before modern preachers is to let go this obsolete
obligation to be the detached voice of authority and instead to claim the
freedom to switch stances, viewpoints and focus so that the consciousness
created by the sermon is at least as broad and varied as the TV programme
that people could have stayed home to watch. But staying home not
surprisingly is what people increasingly do, for who wants to stand locked
in one spot, when there's a whole world to move around in, constantly on
offer by the mass media.

These then are the elements of a preacher's rhetorical strategy to be
considered move by move. To ignore any one of them is to shortchange
the power of the sermon to be a vehicle of grace, just as contemporary as
any latest electronic model.

6
Demythologizing the Mass Media

It's a murky world to most church people. Anonymously owned, profit-driven, electronically generated, unashamedly secular and cynical about anything sacred. Mass media are an alien environment for the church and the few notable exceptions have generated as much scandal as sympathy.

Yet those same media have taken over many of the social roles held by the preacher in particular and the church in general. It's TV commentators and radio personalities more often than bishops and pastors who tell us who we are and where to look for saints and sinners. It's the daily diet of news bulletins that shapes our view of what's most urgent, important and attractive. And it's the programmes we watch for fun that reveal our deepest sympathies.

Surprising, then, that the twentieth-century church has paid so little heed to mass media. The attitude has usually been to ignore it or uncritically buy into it, as we've seen in the American electronic church scene.

The uncritical acceptance approach reflects a wider cultural attitude of treating mass media as all-powerful in their ability to shape events and direct history. Little wonder then that media people seem to enjoy public veneration.

If enough people believe in this almost omnipotent power of the media, there's no end to what media managers can do.

Press barons like William Randolph Hearst exploited that power in attempts to start and stop wars. In times of national emergency, it's the media that must be enlisted first, forcibly if necessary. The control of the UK press during the Falklands war is only the latest in a long series that reflect a great fear of uncontrolled media that weren't properly aligned with the national interest.

Modern mass media studies, however, have begun to challenge that belief in endless power and influence. The older cause and effect analyses that sought to show a single result of a media action (especially if the result involved delinquency, pornography or crime) are being replaced by studies that stress the power of the wider social context to shape attitude and behaviour. Research is increasingly discredited if it distances or divorces the media from the everyday living, working, spending culture of the people who absorb the programmes and products, and the economics and ideologies of those who control them. "The real power of media is located in existing structures of social relationship and systems of culture and belief."[1]

Such a stance makes media effects research more difficult of course. No longer can we blame or praise the media in any straightforward way for what happened in Vietnam and Watergate, the aftermath to the Mt Erebus disaster or the Ethiopian famine. The simple effects theory of media analysis played a large role earlier this century in everything from wartime recruitment and military morale-boosting to the growth of the advertising industry itself. That theory now has given way to the approaches we've already described in our earlier section on models and theory, namely those that stress the cultural context of the process and the nature of communication as a non-stop negotiation of shared meanings between sender and receiver. Contexts can cancel out the power of mass media, receivers can turn media messages upside down. Mass media are not like 007 with an unqualified licence to woo and kill. The difference they make when they make any difference at all is the result of a much more subtle and complex exercise. Any critique of mass media, especially if it's theologically informed, suffers from a scattergun approach. The target is so huge, our critical resources are so small and the focus of our aim is so limited. Most Christian critiques usually settle for a moralistic comment, ignoring completely the deeper structural questions.

Our SMCRF circle offers one way of avoiding that pitfall. For mass media, as opposed to individual or small group communication, there are three features of the circle that change dramatically as the media become "mass-ive".

The receiver is seen from the start not only in relation to a network of primary groups as the Riley model shows, but also as a corporate rather than an individual entity, a market rather than a person.

---

[1] Media-contexts of study, units 1 and 2, Open University, 1977 (a third level course in mass communication and society), pp.39f. The Open University material is available from P.O. Box 48, Milton Keynes, UK MK7 6AB.

The old jokes about the people with 2.5 children, owning one-third of a house, and getting divorced every seven years are taken literally by mass media marketers. The target of their programming is just such an amalgam of norms, trends and averages; a kind of statistical trawl net, stitched together in the hope that at least a part of each of us will be caught up in the sweep. And because the receiver takes on this corporate character, collective factors like the morale, group loyalty and tradition, the influence of external events (such as weather, economic and political stability) on this corporate body takes on new significance.

Davison in his work on media effects[2] attempts to gather these receiver variables together under four crucial conditioners of any audience — personality and educational differences distinctive to the group; the social context and coherence of the group; the external events affecting the group; and the strength of established attitudes held within the group. The last is especially important in planning any change via mass media.[3] Strategies that don't in some way respect and reinforce existing attitudes are doomed to failure, as Abbey's notion of contemporary axioms discussed earlier also showed.

Attitude strength is directly related to another factor mentioned earlier — namely the level of knowledge within a receiver group. Davison quotes several surveys that show media impact on a specified issue was heavily dependent on the level of information already present in the group, and while media programming could develop and strengthen that level, it could do little by itself to plant new information. In fact, there was no direct relationship between exposure, however frequent, to new material and its absorption. One classic case study concerned a 1948 media blitz in Cincinnati, Ohio, providing information about the United Nations. It had minimal impact on a population which had little, if any, previous introduction to the UN.

Because the receiver has to be this depersonalized construct, feedback becomes an elusive element to track down and measure. It's hard enough to be precise about the response of one or two people. To describe the feedback from one or two million becomes a needle-in-the haystack exercise. Market researchers can of course measure how many more bottles of detergent were sold following a TV advertising campaign, and

---

[2] *Mass Media: Systems and Effects,* W. Phillips Davison, Jas. Boylan and Frederick T.C. Yu, New York, Praeger, 1976, Ch. 6.
[3] *Ibid.,* p.179.

through the science of psychographics some broadbrush generalities can match some sorts of people with some sorts of life-style and consumption patterns. But there the feedback measurements must end, for any description of me that depends on what sort of detergent, or deodorant, or TV programme or car or anything else I buy, drive, wear or watch makes a laughably incomplete statement about my humanity or moral values or anything else important. In fact, the TV detergent ad may well be reducing my humanity and eroding my moral values by triviality and distraction.

Channel (or medium) is the third feature of the SMCRF circle that takes on new significance when applied to mass media. The more mass-directed the communication process becomes, the more autonomous the channel becomes, especially if it is dependent on high technology. Electronic mediums such as satellite-linked television or computerized printing operations become self-justifying and self-contained entities in which the demand to keep the technology running profitably limits the freedom of the sender to choose and shape the message.

Mass media channels are made up of a series of filters, each of which in turn influences the messages that pass through. The filters range from mechanical issues of timetable, pay rates, maintenance needs, etc. to professional and legal issues of controlling the content, priorities and standards of messages to economic issues of profit and loss, and the demands of advertisers, audiences and owners. The Hub model best illustrates this multi-layered character of the channel that seems to take on a life of its own.

In order to challenge or change a mass media message it is more often a matter of addressing separate elements within the channel (such as the political loyalties of a journalists' union or the state of the libel laws) than any simple and direct appeal to the media owner. Making changes to the channel, in other words, becomes more important than changing the intentions of the sender.

If direct cause and effect patterns and a simple changing of message won't bring results in mass media, we need to separate the roles that such media do play and for each role develop appropriate strategies for change. Drawing on the pioneering work of Halloran and McQuail, a summary of essential roles would include:

Reality endorsing: By directing our attention, selecting and shaping the problems to be posed, choosing the images that will focus our interest, mass media build a culture of consensus. Whatever receives prominence and repetition becomes more normal, natural, reliable and "real" than that which is seen infrequently or with difficulty. In this way, world-views are made and maintained.

A survey of the UK press coverage of race-related issues from 1963-70[4] illustrates just how much is at stake in this reality-defining role. There were many ways of discussing race, but the press consistently chose to link it with immigration (and all the attendant fears of the majority white culture losing power and influence).

The survey sample showed 2000 column inches devoted to immigration issues, while only 246 column inches covered race-related questions on education, 239 on housing, 206 on unemployment and 97 on stories highlighting racial harmony.

The selection of visual images is an even more subtle way of defining our reality. Consider the selection of pictures used to introduce TV news programmes. Invariably they portray conflict, violence and confrontation. This is the way the world is, we're being told implicitly, so treat the hyped-up stories that follow as representative. Expect all tennis players to have McEnroe-type tantrums, all Arabs to be oil-rich and hijack-eager, all Maori people to be angry and all clergy to be faintly ridiculous. In this way we get used to treating some people as always problematic, some issues as inevitable.

Priority setting: Closely allied to reality-defining, this role never involves saying yes/no, good/bad, but only first, second, third, implying of course that there is solid unity of interest, common mind and purpose behind the choice. It is this role that makes the instruments of headline summary, information bulletin and newsletter so potent. Under the guise of information-only, they are in fact setting priorities by what they leave out as much as what they include. The current media preoccupation with economic issues is a case in point. A shift in the cost price index guarantees coverage, unlike rise and fall in industrial accidents, church attendance, child health statistics. The problem is not simply that such choices are made but rather that they are made without acknowledgment or accountability.

Boundary-lining: The third in this cluster of roles draws the lines for us on who is, culturally speaking, insider and outsider. In crude form, it employs labels like foreign devils, traitor, communist, pagan, etc. but mass media are rarely allowed to be that crass. The more potent sorting is done by drawing the lines between what's reasonable and extreme, where

---

[4] Open University, *op. cit.*, Unit 14. Other units, 7, 13, 15 in particular, provide detailed analysis of media roles and their political impact.

exceptions and special cases are deserved, who is deviant and who is mainstream — Michael Hill[5] has shown the New Zealand media's fascination with sectarian groups, that is quite disproportionate to their size or influence. The gang scene reflects the same syndrome. Gang houses with high walls and fences draw great media consternation whereas the far more elaborate and effective security measures taken by wealthy landowners in select areas of Queenstown or Coromandel draw little or no comment.

Push all or any of these three roles to the extreme and they become exercises in propaganda. It's only a matter of degree, for as Hugh Rank very graphically portrays,[6] propaganda involves intensifying our virtue and down-playing the vices of others. It works in a very subtle way by linking and repeating some ideas, omitting and distracting attention from others, in order to shift boundaries, reorder priorities and refocus our view of the world.

Social integration: One common effect of the three roles listed so far is to create a sense of social stability and coherence for those who have been included and approved by the media's portrayal of the world. (For those excluded, of course, the media's role is experienced as alienation.)

In their own right, mass media channels are major channels of socialization, through which we all, and our children most of all, learn how to live in and what to expect from the world.

Although the media are usually blamed for offending and upsetting equilibrium, singling out exceptions instead of the rule, their major role is nevertheless to build consensus and integration. The already privileged set the terms of that consensus, and the more profit-oriented and technologically dependent the medium, the more careful they will be to ensure the consensus they build is safe and acceptable.

This is not to suggest that individual media can't and don't sometimes produce brave, crusading material. It is only to say that their dominant role is a socially conserving and safeguarding one, more often concerned with slowing down social change than speeding it up.

A 1984 study by the World Association for Christian Communication (WACC), surveying mass media impact on 12,000 households in rural India over a six-year period, showed clearly that these media (radio, books, newspapers) have little influence on social change, except to consolidate the status quo and the interests of the already privileged.

---

[5] *Shades of Deviance*, eds Hill et al., Dunmore, 1983, ch. 9.
[6] *The New Languages*, Olgren and Berk, Prentice Hall, 1977, pp.118f.

Meanwhile the poorer 95% of India's population become relatively more underprivileged even as the impact of mass media on the whole society increases. The really important determinants of social change, the survey concludes, are "interpersonal communication, community activism and political agitation", in that order.

The WACC study believes that its findings, even though drawn from a third-world setting, are being reflected in first-world settings as well, where new research shows the "limited usefulness of mass media as vehicles of social change."[7]

Such a study reinforces the view that mass media function to protect and reinforce the status quo. It's a point we'll need to develop further when deciding just how useful a vehicle mass media provide for a gospel committed to challenging and overturning the status quo.

To discover who benefits most from this social integration that the media so powerfully provide is only part of the analysis. That integrating role is dependent on another media function — the provision of *collective symbols*. These shape all our perceptions, whether or not those symbols best serve our interests. And that's the ambiguity. Our map of the world and its landmarks is constantly being selected for us, regardless of our personal theological or political choices. The values of a profit-driven, consumer culture must dominate when programme choices are dependent on advertising revenue. We can pick and choose between symbols on media offer, but the variety and breadth of our choice are firmly defined by the economic dictates of a mass market system.

That leaves us with the options of either turning off and shutting down all the media channels around us or developing strategies of critical resistance that not only decode the messages, but also recode them into less demanding and defining statements than the mass media managers intend them to be. Such tactics can form strategies of resistance that deflate, divert and rework the dominant symbols. But whatever the strategy, it needs to recognize the pervasive influence of media symbols and rituals, whether or not we enjoy and endorse what they're saying. We may have never been near a rugby ball or sailed even a "P" class dinghy, but All Blacks and 12-metre yachts are media-shaped symbols that define who we are as New Zealanders. Our culture is organized around such collective symbols of identification.

The integrative power of the media depends on its ability to throw up such symbols and hold them before us, again and again, like electronic

---

[7] *Lutheran World Information*, 37/84, p.7.

mantras. Communities of interest sprout up overnight around such symbols and we find ourselves able to relate to people who otherwise would never have crossed our path. It is from such symbols that the rituals and myths that undergird our culture are woven, unstated and unconscious though they are. So, far from being the last in a list of roles, this social integration through symbols function of mass media becomes an all-embracing and all-important category for understanding the difference media make to the way we live.

But however carefully we might analyze such roles, our competence in understanding mass media will constantly be tested by people who expect us to say exactly what effect it has. The cause and effect theories may well be outdated as we've seen, but the expectation that made them so popular remains.

Something that occupies such a massive investment of our time and other people's money as media, that takes such a conspicuous place in our living rooms and on our breakfast tables *must* be making a difference to who we are and what we value. So explain it!

The hunch that media have such power is surely still sound. "There isn't anything that isn't something," as D.H. Lawrence once said, and anything as pervasive as media must really be something.

But the temptation to claim precision about that "something" has to be resisted if all we've said so far is even half true.

The integrity of media studies, to say nothing of their value for the church, depends on *not* joining the chorus of those who see media power alone as able to bring in the kingdom, stop people smoking or fighting or whatever. Such campaigning ends in media idolatry, not analysis, and promotes a false impression of how mass media operate.

What's needed instead is awareness of the small pieces that make up the media picture. In that way the inflated importance we give to media will be broken, the expectations we attach to it will be more realistic and the chances of our criticism or support of particular media issues being heard will be greatly increased.

7
Strategy

So far we've covered some basic ways of understanding how communication happens, and how it can be described and critiqued. But (with the exception of the homiletics chapter) our interest has been in analyzing rather than applying this knowledge. What can be said then about building strategies for effective communication? The variety of contexts for such strategies, even if they are all church-related, is enormous, so any strategy-building advice can only be put in the form of questions.

The ones that follow don't address the technological issues about design and hardware and distribution networks. Our strategy questions cover more basic issues such as who we think we are and what do we think we're doing.

Where do we start from?

Do we see ourselves as part of some established communication system, willing to buy into its terms of reference and style of operating? If so, how far? Is unquestioning loyalty needed to make our communication effective? Would an alternative be better, seeking out channels and styles that are more appropriate, affordable, sustainable, participatory?

Every communication strategy involves elements of one or all three roles of entrepreneur (join the system and make it work for you), alternative (withdraw and set up a better system), or critic (stay with the status quo but seek to reform and change it from inside). How these roles are chosen will set your stance to the strategy questions that follow.

Defining the task and setting the goals

What is it really that we are seeking to do? To change an attitude, behaviour, to redirect attention? Or simply to prepare for such a change, as a preliminary exercise. And is the goal we set something substantial or simply an appearance? To use the language of consumerism, is our interest in the product or its packaging? Michael Traber puts it this way:

> A church does not become part of the public agenda because its public relations officer has produced a press release. This is only possible if a church takes up an issue which affects people's daily lives and is seen to affect their daily lives.[1]

The most significant communication event created by the World Council of Churches in recent times was its Programme to Combat Racism's grants to liberation movements. That action, though small in financial terms, had far more effect than any attempt to market the WCC by starting from its corporate image rather than its programmatic activity.

Who is it for? (and where are they at?)

The advertising industry has proved the importance of knowing precisely who you want to address and finding out all you can about them. Through the science of psychographics, advertising agencies profile everything about a given audience from personality type to social attitudes and values along with more obvious demographic indicators of address, age, income, education, gender, etc.

The church growth movement has shown a similar interest by applying McGavran's "homogenous unit" principle. Despite the original vagueness of that principle, it can be refined and made precise as the advertising industry has done so profitably. What's more, to gather such sociological knowledge of an audience does not commit us to the theological error of building exclusive faith communities of like-minded people, defined more by social class than faith conviction.

So who are we talking to *primarily*, even if many others will overhear? What do they know already? What are the symbols and operative images that work for them?

What channels are available and appropriate?

It's a fine line between defining the target audience and their channels, as the last two questions suggest. For every group or community is organized and defined by the communication channels and networks it employs and trusts. Identifying these channels and the gatekeeper figures that control them, formally from pulpits and editorial desks, informally

---

[1] "The Illusion of 'Mission as Marketing'", *The Ecumenical Review*, Vol. 39, No. 3, July 1987.

over background fences and across corner dairy counters, is the first step in building any communication strategy. The concept of "network" from communication and marketing theory relates closely to McGavran's "homogenous unit" though it can be defined more precisely. For example, evangelist Ray Bakke makes a distinction between rural and urban networks in this way:

> Behind the concept of networking there is a communications theory. I explain it this way: In the rural areas, every relationship is a primary one, and in primary relationships you invest emotion. You are intricately related to wood, because you cut it and burn it, and heat is an emotional experience for you. You know the town drunkard by name; you are known as a part of your family network, and the house where you live: "Oh, you're from the Bakke house." Everybody knows you. In a city, virtually every relationship is a secondary relationship in which you don't invest emotion.
>
> There is a phenomenon that social psychologists have called the concept of overload. It works this way: in a large city, often ten people will be in an elevator, yet no one will speak, because everybody has "space" around him, and if you start speaking, intuitively you sense that you're invading other people's space. So you don't even have to be told not to speak. You just keep quiet. So how do you break through? How do you communicate? You look for *networks*. And there are all kinds of networks. The larger the city, the more diverse they are and the more networks you've got.
>
> Evangelism for me is having people identify their networks. I have them make three charts in my evangelism classes — a biological chart of their extended family, a geographical chart, and a vocational chart — each of the three primary networks. In that chart, they've got anywhere from ten to fifty people. Biological means the people related to you, like Aunty Molly; geographical are the people you live near — your mechanic, your barber, your child's teacher; vocational is the office, the school, the apartment.
>
> In the city I am convinced that, generally speaking, as you move through the classes through middle class to upper middle to upper class, the vocational network is the key network for evangelism. Now, that is one of the realities of urban life, and politics being the art of the possible, the way you get things done is by networking, by creating networks. In fact the simple definition of power, which I believe is accurate, is the ability to get something done. That's power. It's called clout. I don't think it's negative. So, if you're going to move a city, you have to create a network, you have to create an influence and structure.[2]

While people networks are themselves channels (of power in Bakke's sense), channel also has a more technical association, as in video screen

---

[2] *Together Magazine*, January-March 1984, p.31.

or printed page, each of which has distinctive advantages and disadvantages, as this check list from the World Association for Christian Communication shows.

WHAT MEDIA CAN AND CANNOT DO

Advantages	*Disadvantages*

PRINT

Material inexpensive (paper/ink)	Static
Production process simple/rapid	May be hard to distribute
Distribution can be controlled	May be discarded before being read
Long life, permanent referral possible	Can easily be dull
Subject can be dealt with in variety of ways	
Range of illustrative possibilities	
Quick to complete	
Can be done by one person	

MAGAZINES

Selected audience	Deadlines may be months in advance
Frequently affluent audience	Placements may be difficult to obtain
Prestigious	Duplication of circulation may occur
Pass along readership	Market is unlikely to be local
Use of colour and visuals	

NEWSPAPERS

Geographically focused	Short message life
Relatively low cost	Placements are limited, may be difficult to obtain
Reach all income groups	No editorial control
Deadlines for copy relatively short	High cost for national coverage
	Message often sensationalized

DIRECT MAIL

Highly selective audience	Poor image of junk mail
Message can be personalized	Difficult to maintain good lists
Easy to provide means for reader action (return envelopes, etc.)	Expensive and time-consuming to produce good mailings
Competition is not directly with other advertisers	Postage is expensive and heavily regulated

PAMPHLETS AND BROCHURES

Detailed message	Deadlines may be long for printing and production
Future reference	
Thoughtful presentation and distribution enhanced	Production costs and time may be high
Many possible formats and colours	Effectiveness difficult to measure unless coupon is used
May be directed to select audience	Audience wants classy production but often resents high cost

BROADCAST TV

High quality production	Shotgun audience, all audiences indiscriminately
Large audience	

Advantages

Impressive authenticity, credibility
People relate readily to it
Visual possibilities
Demonstrability, presence
Unrealized creative, artistic and communicational potential

VIDEO TAPE
Easy to learn/exciting medium
Inexpensive (compared to broadcast)
Tape is reusable
Instant playback
Portable equipment
Involves many people

RADIO
Inexpensive to produce
Creative use of music and effects
Low cost and accessible receiving equipment
Relatively easy to get air time
Applicable for groups and individuals
Some selectivity of audience
Good saturation of local markets
Easy to alter copy, edit, adapt, update
Great creative access to the imagination

FILM
Large audience potential
Powerful creative art form
Playback equipment relatively inexpensive and available
Involves many people
Both audio and visual

SLIDE/TAPE
Inexpensive to produce
Can be used with large or small group
Easily revised
Equipment available
Familiar medium: anyone can use almost anywhere
Involves many people
Communicate a specific idea or impression to a specific audience
Entertains and uses pictures and words to convey concepts and ideas
An omniscient narrator and/or experts convey message, enhance credibility

Disadvantages

Requires excessive time and production expense
Difficult to get into
Air time is costly if paid for
Future referral to message is difficult
Message limited by short segments, commercial interruptions and context

Still somewhat expensive
Playback limited to small groups
Broadcast quality requires further investment
Lack of consistent compatible hardware and formats in the industry
Spoiled by broadcast TV
People expect too much

Needs quiet surroundings
No visual message
Hard to get cohesive public due to variety of listening habits
May only be heard marginally as people do other things
Message limited by short segments
Difficult to refer back to the message
Audience still often too broad

Expensive to produce and duplicate
Long time in production
Formal, final quality, with less process and feedback
Hard to edit or change

More elaborate presentation may require tricky, expensive equipment
Audience tends to drift away
Audience easily distracted
Difficult to convey a lot of information
Cannot be longer than 10-15 minutes without boring or confusing the audience
The audience cannot easily refer back to the show for clarification of facts
Alterations may be costly
Funds, facilities and skills are required to produce a show
Slide shows and film strips have acquired a negative "schoolish" image in the last ten years

A further level of channel choice is offered by the (Abbey's) concept of contemporary axioms described earlier, whereby every established communication vehicle, be it "Women's Weekly" or football club bar, quickly gathers around it (and eventually institutionalizes) firm expectations about what you expect to hear and say in that context.

The golden rule about channels and networks, and the reason for labouring the point about how carefully we need to identify them, is never to create new ones where existing ones can be borrowed and used. For every channel has to have a life, personality, tradition and style of its own to win credibility and that is only won after much time and pain. The trouble with one-off evangelistic events is just that they try to create an instant channel and produce, not surprisingly, one-off experiences, which might be fun, but hardly qualify as vehicles for a faith that not only turns your life around but also keeps it headed in a new direction.

Finally, there are some very practical questions of what channels are available, affordable, sustainable on the economy of scale that most churches work within. Photocopy machines and cassette tapes have revolutionized the cost of some communication technology but most commercially controlled mass media channels still remain outside church access.

Why me/us?

This is the strategy question most often taken for granted, which is why preachers find it so hard to share their pulpits. But on this subject, with this audience, on this occasion, in this cultural context, with this age or gender group, in an age where the authority of any speaker cannot be taken for granted, we increasingly have to ask whose voice, face, presence or pen is most appropriate. The channel we represent, new or established, may well be the wrong one here, this time. By speaking without checking, we may well be guaranteeing non-communication before we open our mouths. For by speaking, who will we be seen to be competing with, rather than complementing? The ecumenical movement this century has helped denominational churches realize that an increasingly sceptical world has seen them to be talking at and past each other, sometimes across the same street corner, even when the churches themselves thought they were saying very different and vitally important things. Today in a culture that checks the race, sex, age, appearance and individuality of each speaker very carefully before switching on and tuning in, the odds are that someone other than the one you take for granted might be better placed to do the talking or writing.

Alongside and against that heightened discernment of who-best-speaks-where are the patterns of selectivity formed by habit and familiarity. Mass media are a conservative enterprise. We trust the newsreader and the actor we know before the brilliant outsider. On the day I wrote this, I spent my lunchtime browsing through a bookshop. The only religious title on the display shelves in this most contemporary of shops was a life of Christ by Charles Dickens, of all people. A Victorian novelist, famous, though not for his theological insight, is the only Christian voice that the economics of publishing could include in this secular display. Not because of his competence but rather because he was familiar and trusted enough to write (and sell) about anything. A book by Dickens on goldfish breeding would have been equally acceptable. So "Why me?" — "Because they know me" may be a good place to start, even if only to let you say "Here's someone else I'd like you to meet."

Is anybody listening? (and if so, what are they hearing?)

This most obvious of questions is added with great reluctance to most church-related communication strategies. More often than not, it's added too late to influence the process anyway, so people quickly become cynical about filling in evaluation sheets that aren't going to change anything anyway.

Effective strategies need to make space for feedback gathering early enough to influence the next step. And remembering the multi-levelled nature of feedback, it needs to be checked and rechecked with time between for reflection and re-appraisal. Week after week in our churches, sermons are preached, newsletters distributed, announcements made. And on the basis of only the sketchiest, hearsay impression these strategies are repeated in the same form next week. Further, such impressions are also highly selective in the sense that they rely more on verbal than visual clues. Empty pews don't count as much as angry voices or letters. A sharp question at a parish AGM strikes home better than the familiar visual evidence of an aging congregation where younger faces drop in and don't return. We hear what we want to hear and if we fear that people might not be listening, we're inclined not to ask.

Returning to our original circular model of the communication process, we've asked strategy questions of each element of the circle:

Sender	— why me/us?
Channel	— what's available and appropriate?
Receiver	— who are they, where are they at?
Response	— how seriously is feedback seen and used?

We don't however have a strategy question attached to message. Deliberately so, for the message we can offer (and it's offer rather than send or dictate) is entirely dependent on all the other strategy questions listed from understanding and respect for the receiver, through to who we think we are as senders. The message, however noble, eternally true and inspired we believe it to be, is an idle issue to discuss alone in communication terms, separate from all the other elements of the circle. For where we haven't sown we can't reap; where we haven't invested we can't earn; where we haven't won trust and respect we can't conjure it up. There is nothing magic about the communication process, *even* if, especially if, the message we offer is held to be divinely spoken. The cost of credible communication is built into the way the world is. It's a cost that even God has to pay, which is what Christ's incarnation is all about. In our next chapter we say why.

8
Evangelism

What's the point of studying Christian communication if it doesn't lead to winning souls and growing churches? By that view the value of all we've said so far hangs on the adequacy of this chapter, for when words like evangelism, mission and church growth enter the conversation, expectations soar. In an age and culture as pragmatic, success-oriented and cost-effective as ours, to talk evangelism is to talk about the measurable difference faith makes. And if the difference is *only* one of deeper understanding and clearer discernment rather than an increase in numbers and budgets then disappointment is guaranteed for some, so polarized is the debate over what we mean by these words.

What do we mean by evangelism? Bill Adams of Australia's Uniting Church makes a useful list of what evangelism is not.[1] It does not require us to all talk about conversion continually, to follow the same style of mission, to increase the numerical size of our churches, to all have the same kind of religious experience, to place ourselves over against the world, to choose between evangelism and something else like social justice or liturgical renewal. Such suggestions are false choices, diverting us from the variety of activities and approaches that evangelism has classically encompassed. What makes evangelism distinctive is not some (usually verbal and aggressive) style, or some (usually spectacular) results, but rather the proclamation of the good news of Jesus Christ.

A comprehensive statement that spells out that brief definition in terms of calling to repentance, announcing forgiveness and new beginning is found in the WCC's 1983 "Mission and Evangelism — an Ecumenical Affirmation". In terms of communication theory it's the deliberate, intentional announcing and offering of that good news, so as to offer an

---

[1] *CCA News,* 15 November 1988, p.12.

invitation, pose a choice and expect a response that gives focus to the word. Some other things follow from this offering-response understanding to make it credible. It should be seen, like all communication events, as an ongoing process. The question is not "Are you saved?" but "Are you being saved?" And unless there is some provision from the outset for that question to be continually asked and the answers heard then the process is quickly reduced to a one-off, one-time action.

Evangelism is an area of urgency and choice, often corporate, always personal. It's the high-risk mode of Christian speaking because it takes the chance of being rejected. As such it raises the stakes and sharpens all the questions we've already covered in communication theory. Respect and acceptance of the receiver, care in hearing his/her response, cultural sensitivity over the choice of appropriate channels, continuity with what is already known and understood — all these criteria become crucial in whether responses are made that will change lives and communities. Acceptance — saying yes — after all, is only one early stage in the stages of feedback that lead to action of the turn-around-start-all-over-again kind involved in true conversion.

Evangelism in this sense forms the core of the church's mission — the wider task that God has set for the church in the world. Evangelism enlists people for that mission by calling them to Christ, in order to get on with the job of loving and serving.

When evangelism ends with or even lingers over the experience of encountering Christ, then the gospel is degraded. For as Karl Barth reminded us: "What makes a person a Christian is not primarily his or her personal experience of grace and redemption, but his or her ministry... It is not simply to receive life that people are called to become Christians, but rather to give life... whenever the church's involvement in society becomes secondary and optional, whenever the church invites people to take refuge in the name of Jesus without challenging the dominion of evil, it becomes a countersign of the kingdom."[2]

What kind of life should evangelism give? The church growth movement has some clear answers to that question, so clear that evangelism and church growth are increasingly used as interchangeable terms.

Peter Wagner of Fuller Seminary, and the first incumbent of the Chair of Church Growth at that school, says that "anyone who does not accept the McGavran paradigm is not a church growth person".[3] He is referring

---

[2] Quoted in David Bosch, *International Bulletin of Missionary Research*, July 1987, p.102.
[3] *Church Growth Magazine*, Vol. 2, No. 2, March-April 1985, p.190.

to the work of Donald McGavran whose book *Understanding Church Growth*[4] is definitive for that movement. Based on his experience as a missionary in India, McGavran argues for a "finding" rather than "seeking", a "discipling" as well as a "perfecting" theology. He urges the use of sociological and anthropological analysis in evangelism, notably the principle of the "homogenous unit" whereby people are sought in groups (tribes, castes, communities etc.) rather than individuals. "The main problem", says McGavran, "is how to present Christ so that men can truly follow him without traitorously leaving their kindred."[5]

By applying that principle among Indian castes, McGavran saw some spectacular results, and launched a tide of followers and critics. Wayne McClintock, a New Zealand missionary sociologist working with Interserve, argues that the homogenous unit principle is too vague to be useful outside its original context.[6] When defined as no more than a group with "some characteristic in common", the principle becomes so elastic as to be meaningless, leaving each church planter free to establish his or her own criteria. By glossing over complex social realities, such as religious adherence and economics, "a neatly packaged standardized approach to mission" is produced, argues McClintock. He believes the church growth school is headed for obsolescence unless this fundamental weakness in the sociology it uses is addressed.

Even more obvious problems with the church growth methodology surface in the simplistic generalizations about what fosters and stunts growth. You can find this out, evidently, by checking on such evidence as the titles in the minister's library, whether or not he attended Bible college and the frequency of "signs and wonders" in the congregation. Such check lists caricature McGavran's vision. They do not respect the

DIMENSIONS

Qualities	Numerical	Organic	Conceptual	Diaconal
Spirituality				
Incarnational				
Faithfulness				

[4] Grand Rapids, Wm. B. Eerdmans, 1970.
[5] *Ibid.*, p.191.
[6] *International Review of Mission*, Vol. LXXVII, No. 305, January 1988.

multi-dimensional nature of growth that Latin American evangelical writer Orlando Costas[7] has laid out in a guide that interconnects all these variables. Growth involves all these dimensions linking together.

Charles Bayer, author of *A Guide to Liberation Theology for Middle Class Congregations*,[8] writing in *Christian Ministry Magazine*, believes:

> Church growth ideas provide a marvellous set of productive membership recruitment disciplines. But it is not evangelism. It is, in fact, the trivialization of evangelism. Approaching people who are very much like us and convincing them that they should join our ranks may be a wise sales strategy, but it is not the proclamation of the evangel. Church growth does not necessarily entail evangelism, and increasing membership in the institutional church may not necessarily result in building the kingdom. This scheme can well be counter-productive to the gospel's power for radical transformation. If we are called to be unlike the once-born, bringing more of them in simply will not re-create in Christ's image either them or us.
>
> The problem we face is not the lack of evangelistic techniques, but the loss of the evangel. Ours is not an organizational problem, it is a theological problem. But God has not left us without a witness. God has provided the poor to be our teachers. It is through them that we can recover both the evangel and the meaning of evangelism.
>
> Liberation theology has taught us that evangelism is the fruit of Christian praxis. It has little to do with getting people to join our churches. That is only one possible result of evangelism, and not the most important one at that. It is God who adds to the church those who are being saved (Acts 2:47b). When we are faithful to the gospel, God may increase our numbers. In a society openly hostile to the radical message of the gospel, we should not expect the church to win popularity contests. Every congregation must ask itself whether it is ready to take that risk.[9]

Bayer ends his article with this haunting story:

> An hour's drive from Beijing stands the magnificent summer residence of Tz'u-hsi, also known as the Empress Dowager, who dominated the Chinese empire in the latter half of the 19th century. The summer palace was the site of enormous garden parties for the elite of the Ch'ing dynasty. Now it belongs to the people, who visit it by the millions, all looking around proudly as if to say, "This is mine now." In the centre of the estate is a lake, once the home of the Chinese navy. Tz'u-hsi was told that unless she rebuilt the fleet, China would

---

[7] "A Wholistic Concept of Church Growth", in *Experiencing Church Growth*, ed. Wilbert Shenk, Grand Rapids, Wm. B. Eerdmans, 1983, p.105.

[8] CBP Press, 1986.

[9] January-February 1988, p.7.

not be safe from her traditional enemies. Ironically, she commissioned only one ship — made of concrete. It was really a pier jutting out from the cluster of elegant buildings on the lake's shoreline. Its purpose was to host extravaganzas for the nobles of the land, who flocked to it in great numbers.

The church is Christ's navy, commissioned both to search the sea for the shipwrecked and to make the ocean a safer place for those who sail on it. Massive, immobile concrete ships, sitting in tranquil inland lakes and built for the enjoyment of "our kind of people", may enliven the scenery, but they offer nothing to the drowning.

What positive contribution has the church growth movement made to our understanding of evangelism? It's produced some excellent pastoral advice of the sort we always knew but never got around to saying out loud. Like the fact that 85% of those who attend church do so because someone befriended them, like seeing that small groups work better than big ones, and that churchgoers form sub-cultures, different from non-churchgoers.

The movement has also alerted and challenged mainstream churches in the liberal tradition who smugly took their continued future for granted. As patterns of biological growth have collapsed, these churches have been helped out of their slumber by the church growth debate, to ask what sort of church they need to be to survive, before the sign goes up on the door, "Last one out turn off the light".

The question at its deepest level is an ecclesiological one, about the shape of the church community. The church growth model is unashamedly a gathered one, the fellowship of saints, drawn in from the world, breaking connections with the secular culture, certain that He is with us in the church, not so sure that She is waiting for us to join Her in the world.

Models of a servant church that is little interested in its own survival and internal domestic life except as a base to serve from, or a church that faces outwards to the community in every part of its life, even in the language and symbols of its worship — such models are hard to find in the church growth movement, yet many such churches do exist and grow.

Even rarer in church growth discussions is any mention of a comprehensive model of church. One that doesn't worry too much about who's in and out, that deliberately sits light to the demands and identity of membership and seeks to be continuous with and affirming of the culture around. Such churches understand that being "in the world" is a positive claim and doesn't contradict being "not of the world". The heritage of many mainstream churches is bound up with this now much devalued model which only serves to make the challenge of church growth more painful. Ironically, while the comprehensive model is out of favour and gathered, close-knit, clearly bounded communities are all the rage, such gathered groups are still willing and eager to borrow state-of-the-art strategies and technologies of the secular world, especially of the corporate market place. Even the most culture-condemning congregation happily uses the latest overhead projector to sing its disdain of this world and its longing for the next. The divisions, then, between these models of church are not as neat as they seem.

Even though the church growth movements' ecclesiology and theology are not world-affirming, its insistence that we take our numbers, budgets, corporate planning and institutional futures seriously has a pragmatic, down-to-earth, this-worldly quality about it, often lacking in mainstream churches that profess (but don't practise) a more incarnational theology and a more accepting, open-ended ecclesiology.

Such mainstream churches would be expected for instance to lead in the use of media for evangelism, but instead it's the smaller, conservative churches that have set the pace. Not that there is any clear consensus among church growers. Win Arn, founder of the Institute for American Church Growth, told *Christianity Today* magazine that TV evangelism is a "great failure in persuading people to become Christ's disciples and to be responsible members of the church". He quoted a survey of 40,000 Christians, only .01% of whom said they attended church as a result of mass evangelism, including religious radio and TV.

Compare this negative assessment of media evangelism with the earlier experience of Billy Graham. According to Marshall Frady, Graham's biographer, [10] the "central activating principle of Graham's whole life and ministry was the ultimate significance of the mass-reality". As Graham himself enthusiastically propounded: "By using today's mass communications, we can preach to more people in one day than the Apostle Paul reached in a life-time. I imagine that if Paul could look down here, he is champing at the bit. How he would like to be on television! How he would like to have a radio hour!" Frady comments: "It never seemed to occur to Graham that there might be an existential difference of kind between those two ministries precisely for those reasons." On the contrary, as Graham's former public relations director, Jerry Beavan, once declared: "In our crusades and work, we need every instrument of modern

---

[10] *Billy Graham, a Parable of American Righteousness*, Boston, Little Brown, pp.285f.

mass communications. We've got the greatest product in the world to sell
— salvation for men's souls through Christ. Why shouldn't we sell it as
effectively as we promote a bar of soap?" In Graham's case, it is a mass
evangelism that operates out of the pop-metaphysic that the more, the
truer and mightier. As a Graham advocate has explained: "When the
average, moral, reputable American... sees thousands of respectable,
normal people listening and consenting to all this he hears, and then sees
hundreds voluntarily get up and walk to the front in response... he'll
begin to consider the message and the situation with some sincere, honest
interest. It's much easier to say a single speaker is wrong than to discredit
the conviction and decision of thousands."

Such statements now belong to an earlier age before the Crusadegate
watersheds of media evangelism provided by the Bakke, Swaggert and
Roberts scandals, when media technology promised a taste, if not a whole
slice of the kingdom. The mood now is more cautious but despite that,
church growth movers and shakers are still more ready than other groups
to invest in media technology and know-how to tell their story and offer
their invitation. Just as their music chimes in with the sounds and rhythms
of the surrounding culture, so does their language, style, appearance,
methodology, everything but their theology which is actually saying that
this world in God's eyes is not such a nice place at all.

Which brings us to the heart of the matter faced by every decision about
communication for evangelism, be it from the church growth school or
any other. Are the methods employed and the values evoked consistent
with the gospel conviction about unconditional love, acceptance, forgiveness, justice and service?

You can debate the list of such gospel qualities — as we do in the next
chapter — but there's no dispute about the kind of communication the
gospel doesn't support — anything that manipulates, demeans, bullies or
distorts the humanity of the other; anything in which power is used over,
rather than shared with.

Raymond Fung, evangelism secretary for the WCC, puts it this way:

> The issue is deeply theological: can a person, a missionary society, or a
> church, indeed a whole people, who holds human power over others truly
> evangelize? I think not. If I hold power over others, I can feed them, I can
> protect them. I can impose my will on them or manipulate their will. I can
> instruct them. I can lead them. I can even offer my life for them. But I cannot
> challenge them. As long as I have power over others, I cannot challenge them
> to repent, or to stand up and walk, or to take up one's cross and follow Jesus. I
> can say these words all right, backed by the power I possess. But if I am not

blinded by chauvinism, I could not reasonably hope for any response other than reciprocal manipulation. Or I am simply playing games with people's souls. As long as I hold power over others, I cannot share the gospel of Jesus Christ with them and expect an authentic response. There is no evangelism. There is only proselytism. [11]

Such a statement undermines any attempt to control or coerce anyone in the name of evangelism. The key issue is how and whether "I *hold* power" over others. I may well have *more* power and if any sort of corporate or technological communication system is involved (be it typewriter or TV network) some sort of power advantage will be involved. So the question is never simply the ownership but always the exercise of that power. If it's used for securing my place, and putting you in yours, for protecting my privilege, and limiting yours, then communication credibility dissolves. Put positively, the question becomes whether I'm willing to use my power to enable you to discover your own. The risk of course is that in the process my power may be lost. It will certainly be changed.

Such vulnerability is incredibly hard to institutionalize, plan and budget for. The risk of misusing, even losing power is too great. So evangelism is reduced to an exercise for individuals and small groups. Mass media are increasingly seen as unworkable (let alone unaffordable!) for evangelism. Yet the people furthermost from the church are often most dependent on the media for their values and ideals. Such "secular" people are not literate in the language of Zion, the hallowed symbols of faith don't resonate for them and the traditional figures from the Christian cloud of witnesses are comic if anything, apart from the exceptions that the media themselves have allowed, like Mother Teresa. In a recent UK opinion poll, 100 percent listed pop star Cliff Richard as a well-known Christian, 3 percent mentioned Archbishop of Canterbury Dr Runcie.

It's increasingly clear that only those Christians who are prepared to negotiate anew with the media culture are going to be heard and seen by and through it. To stand on the sidelines or to insist on returning to some earlier agreement is to ensure the gospel is ignored. Evangelism is firmly fixed on the church's corporate agenda. As public body, the church is talking all the time to the world around it, even if it doesn't think it's opening its mouth, as much by what it doesn't say and do as by what it does.

---

[11] WCC's *Monthly Letter on Evangelism*, Nos 4/5, April-May 1986.

9
Communication and Theology

Communication by Christians about Christianity has no special privileges. Even if it uses holy words on holy ground, it is no different from communication by or about anything else in creation. The process is the same. We can attempt a distinctive Christian understanding of communication and say how we see and say it through the eyes and ears of faith. What we can't do is use our faith to claim immunity, exemption, superiority, or exclusivity for our kind of communication.

Unfortunately, much of the debate about communication theology is about seeking such special conditions. Charles H. Kraft[1] lists ten common Christian myths concerning communication:

1. Hearing the gospel with one's ears is equivalent to "being reached" with the gospel.
2. The words of the Bible are so powerful that all people need to bring them to Christ is to be exposed to hearing/reading the Bible.
3. The Holy Spirit will make up for all mistakes if we are sincere, spiritual, and prayerful enough.
4. As Christians, we should severely restrict our contracts with "evil" people and refrain from going to "evil" places lest we "lose our testimony" and ruin our witness.
5. Preaching is God's ordained means of communicating the gospel.
6. The sermon is an effective vehicle for bringing about life change.
7. There is one best way to communicate the gospel.
8. The key to effective communication is the precise formulation of the message.
9. Words contain their meanings.
10. What people really need is more information.

---

[1] *Communication Theory for Christian Witness*, Nashville, Abingdon, 1983, pp.36f.

Most reflect a lack of basic information about communication as a process. Others, like 2,3 and even 5 are supernaturalist, magic, or are built, like 4, on an unacceptably dualistic theology. In cold print these myths are easy to expose. In practice the same myths are still pervasive and powerful, always temptingly within reach when we're asked to explain what makes our communication Christian. And just what is that *Christian* ingredient? At the heart of our answers to that question, some of the following concepts emerge:

— the creative, initiating power and presence of God as Father, Son and Holy Spirit;
— the language of Zion, the breadth and accuracy of the theological and biblical vocabulary;
— the personal worth, sincerity, purity, and fidelity of the disciple;
— the degree to which Jesus is imitated, followed and modelled;
— the truth of what's said and how boldly it's told;
— the quality of the dialogue — how sensitively people are heard and helped to speak;
— the beauty, size and perfection of what's produced;
— the measurable success in producing new understanding and/or attracting greater numbers;
— the usefulness, efficiency and growth potential of what's produced;
— the outcomes for justice, peace, community building;
— the immediate relevance of the experience produced;
— the care and consistency with which tradition is honoured;
— the degree of communication to which we are in communion with others.

These concepts can be grouped under four general headings which form the core of the diagram of page 69.

1. Dialogue

Here the focus is on communication *between* people, built through conversation that builds relationships. So the degree of participation, quality of listening, appropriateness of speaking are still important, within and between individuals, groups and cultures. Hendrik Kraemer[2] sees dialogue as a fundamental theological category and "the hallmark of our humanity, yet more conspicuous by its failure than its success". "The God of the Bible", says Kraemer, "is a God who speaks... who wants personal relationship" and whose history with us is "seen under the angle

---

[2] *The Communication of the Christian Faith*, Cambridge, Lutterworth, 1957.

STARTING POINTS FOR A THEOLOGY OF COMMUNICATION

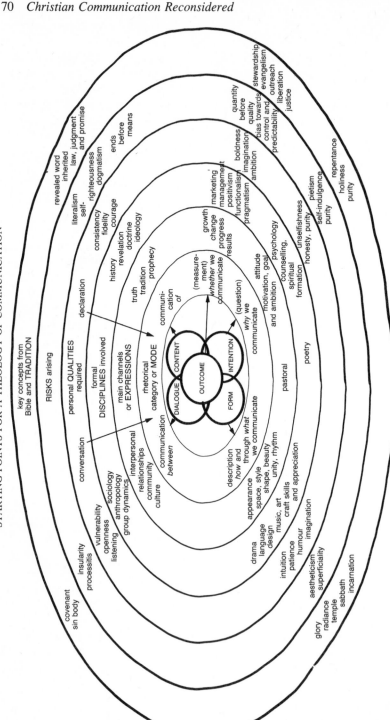

of a continued discourse." God's "love is that state of mutual transparency, disposability and responsiveness in which true communication comes to full fruition".[3]

Fundamental though this dialogue category is, it's easily distorted. Concern for the quality of dialogue can overshadow awareness of who is left out of the conversation, and the wider importance of what's being said. Dialogue can seem very Christian in holy huddles, very meaningful in navel-gazing small groups but very indulgent and irrelevant to everyone else.

The deepest challenge of dialogue at any level from personal to structural lies with the power that has to be shared before true communication can take place. Raymond Fung's words quoted earlier on the impossibility of evangelism happening from any position of superior power apply here equally. In so far as the speaker or sender is willing and able to risk losing control and allow receivers to shape the dialogue, even to reject it, "Christian" communication is taking place.

2. Content

"It's what you say, not how you say it or who you are that counts." Such a view would typify this category, which settles the meaning of "Christian" by *what* we communicate, regardless of how it's communicated. If the Name is named, the Truth proclaimed, and the Word spoken then everything else is secondary. That's overstated, but no more so than fundamentalist groups who measure their communication by the number of times Jesus is mentioned or traditionalist churches who repeat time-hallowed liturgies with an equally mechanical justification. Biblically, the content category is strongly represented by the tradition of prophets who spoke the truth of Yahweh however inadequately and ill-received. They spoke, as Martin Luther said, 2,000 years later, because they could do no other.

3. Intention

The hardest of all categories to discern, and perhaps the most influential, for "I may speak in the tongues of men or angels, but if I am without love, I am a sounding gong or a clanging cymbal" (1 Cor. 13:2). Why we speak, what motivates our words and actions is the deepest test of our communication credibility. The measurement is not the mention of

---

[3] *Ibid.*, pp.15f.

"Lord, Lord", nor our assurance of sincerity, for we are soon seen to protest too much.

The tests we make of each other's intentions in the spiritual realm are more exacting and more subtle. A court of law leaves it to a jury of peers to decide. In the church the process is never that clear which is one reason why the Roman Catholic Church bestows sainthood so cautiously and tardily, long after the event. The current interest in personal spirituality and the rise of pastoral psychology offer a renewed vocabulary for describing intention and motivation, but there are no guarantees that we can communicate, rank or assess it any more precisely than before. That's why poetry is listed alongside psychology as one of the disciplines this category demands.

4. Form

This category looks to the shape and appearance, the unity and rhythm of communication for a clue about its "Christianness". In doing so it gives artistic insight, theological status, trusting that the painter's line, the musician's sound and the writer's image can be divinely revealing. Such a category poses huge problems for traditions reliant on words over pictures and distrustful of sensory and emotive experience. Even so there is biblical evidence aplenty for giving value to form. In the Old Testament God's presence and power is expressed through God's glory, literally radiance *(Kabod)* which is close to our modern word "beauty". In the New Testament, the Good News centres on the human *form* God takes in Jesus. However outrageous and unbecoming, the choice of form said it all, as does God's faithfulness to that form which remained "like us in every way". Being incarnated or embodied in the shapes and rhythms of material creation is the way God works. Judith Rock puts it bluntly:

> In the incarnation, Christians have been directed to physicality and form as the locations of God's presence. The physicality of the incarnation is not, as we are so tempted in our hearts to believe, a temporary inconvenience to divinity. Perhaps it is difficult to believe otherwise because physicality can be such an inconvenience to us. We are clumsy, we get sick, we grow old, we die. Being embodied is often uncomfortable and embarrassing. And so, discovering that we can't escape the oppressive grace-fullness of our bodies, we do what we can to ensure that God, at least, shall escape our pains and frustrations. In how many Christian imaginations and theologies, private and public, does Jesus the Christ swoop through the 33 years of his life, dipping briefly into the world of matter before soaring off toward the real point, the resurrection? Of course, there is his appalling death. But do we not tend, more

often than we care to admit, to see his death as the necessary event that makes the resurrection work?

The message is that the elements of faith — revelation, grace and sacrament — have no meaning, do not work, apart from the physical world and the human talent for form-giving. They are physical events in the ongoing drama in the theatre of revelation. They extend, we believe, beyond the physical world into the mystery of God. One can, they tell us, get there from here. But if one doesn't start here, revel in the here, wrestle in the here, one won't get there.[4]

5. Outcome

This category can connect with all four others. (It also can swallow them up.) The questions this time are: "What difference does your communication make? What results does it produce? Let's take your answer and measure it, in terms of growth achieved, progress made, data collected."

Such a category fits well in a pragmatic climate where cost-effectiveness and management-by-objectives rule. It's also a salutary approach in a church inclined to a she'll-be-right style, unbothered by whether its ministry and mission is reaching anyone new. The outcome category takes seriously the biblical call to human responsibility, stewardship of creation and accountability to God for how we handle the job. Perhaps the great risk it poses is that of using the wrong measurements — of muddling quantity with quality, expecting increased numbers where increased commitment is more appropriate and vice versa. Orlando Costas' growth grid in the chapter on evangelism is a useful way of avoiding this danger of messing up the measurement and thereby missing the point of what's Christian. Outcomes need not of course be measured only in terms of growth in numbers or faithfulness, at one end of the theological spectrum. They can equally be measured by more corporate and harder-to-define criteria of whether the communication creates community, maintains and develops culture and fosters participation, as WACC guidelines have suggested. But the bias of this outcome-centred approach is clearly against such elusive criteria. So easily measured, observed and accessed evidence like head counts, cash totals and bricks and mortar rule the day. Hence the danger of this fifth circle. It can dissolve the value of the other four by insisting that it's only results that count, and anything goes to get them.

---

[4] Judith Rock & Norman Mealy, *Performer as Priest and Prophet*, Harper & Row, 1988.

Conclusion

The scheme presented in the diagram unashamedly renders simple answers impossible to the question "What makes our communication 'Christian'?"

For any one answer could involve crossing all five categories. Reliance on any one category leaves us having to trim and twist our experience of the way God's presence and power is felt and God's leading is received and understood.

What's more, the balance of our choice of categories will alter depending on how corporately or individually communication happens. In mass media communication for example, where dialogue is severely limited, intentions are so easily camouflaged (where do the programmes end and the ads begin?) and content is governed by audience ratings, the form category takes on new importance for judging the gospel value of a programme. Even where the content may be uninspiring, the motivation mixed and the dialogue limited by an on-off switch and volume control, questions of harmony and space (as components of form) can still be positively answered:

> *Harmony:* Are form and purpose considered together? Does the technology involved suit the task, is it sustainable, does it create new dependency? Is the choice of media, length and format suitable for the subject and the audience? Is the item presented with clarity, economy, precision, variety of tone, and sense of humour?
>
> *Space:* Is there room for mystery, risk, reversal and surprise in the communication process being attempted? Is there room left for grace to work its own way? Does the item respect the "otherness" of the gospel by refusing to explain everything, and refusing to judge too easily and quickly? Does the item reflect the gospel's reversal of normal order, importance and value — last before first, foolish before wise, weak before powerful, poor before rich?[5]

Such considerations are gospel issues, every bit as much as whether or not we're kind to each other, generous to charitable causes, careful not to covet other people's spouses, blaspheme, get drunk, and all the other popular ways of measuring "Christian" identity. That same identity in corporate or mass communication may be equally affirmed by leaving space for surprise, respecting doubts, finding mystery and beauty in the midst of the ordinary and ugly, or even by choosing the form of a story that invites response on the listener's terms instead of a sermon that demands answers on the preacher's terms. Finally, we resort to the

---

[5] John Bluck, *Beyond Technology*, WCC, Geneva, 1984, p.19f.

language of piety. Perhaps all that can be said for certain about how Christian our communication is, comes down to how much room we leave for God to move and address us indirectly but personally.

Indirectly, for all Christian communication is mediated communication, incarnated in humanity, Jewish in the model of Mary and Joseph's boy, expressed sacramentally through the day-to-day, food-and-drink stuff of creation.

Personally, because that is the way God always eventually engages us, calling us by our name. Like the demons in the New Testament stories, we find that personal naming and claiming unbearable. So we opt for communication media that disembody and depersonalize, protecting us from the risk of self-disclosure. It's in such a communication arena that being and becoming Christian is hardest of all; where the familiar, the secure and predictable is the order of the day — the monotony of the local newspaper, radio talk-back, TV sitcoms and the chat about the weather on the way to work. Yet it's that communication arena where we spend most of our waking lives and energies. Where the challenge of discipleship is sharpest there we seem to be least confident and equipped as Christian communicators. The church-bound, individualized and moralistic models of theology we've inherited don't help us meet that challenge. Nothing less than a new theological framework is needed. One that starts by valuing our local context as the area of God's active presence and then goes on to ask the sort of questions we've raised in this chapter.